MW01245527

" *Essays to My Daughter* : tions. It will be assigned reading in my classes, but more importantly, it will be the gift I'll send to friends and colleagues. Steven Simpson helps us understand why we care about the natural world."

—DAN GARVEY, PROFESSOR AND PRESIDENT EMERITUS, PRESCOTT COLLEGE

" Such great writing and spirit! In *Essays to My Daughter on Our Relationship With the Natural World*, Steven Simpson smoothly transitions from commonplace occurrences in nature to thoughtful insights about humankind's relationship with the natural world. This is outstanding nature writing. Many of us in Taiwan have enjoyed Simpson's nature writing for decades. Through the conversation with his daughter, he has inspired me to think about experiences in nature more deeply and to pass them down to the next generation."

—HUEI-MIN TSAI, PROFESSOR, GRADUATE INSTITUTE OF ENVIRONMENTAL EDUCATION, NATIONAL TAIWAN NORMAL UNIVERSITY

" Once again, Steve Simpson shows his remarkable capacity to take a philosopher's complex conceptual work—he did as much with Lao Tzu and John Dewey in earlier books—and explain it in rich and uncomplicated language. *Essays to My Daughter on Our Relationship With the Natural World* will be at home on college reading lists and on the coffee tables of those interested in more deeply exploring their relationships with the places and ecosystems they inhabit."

—SIMON BEAMES, PROFESSOR, THE NORWEGIAN SCHOOL OF SPORT SCIENCES

" Like a conversation with a friend, *Essays to My Daughter* is about the formation of an environmental philosophy. Simpson intimately combines his personal experiences with classic nature writing from the likes of Leopold, Thoreau, and Cather. Through one man's wisdom shared with his daughter, this collection has lessons for all future generations as they explore and develop their own relationship with nature."

—LEO MCAVOY, PROFESSOR EMERITUS, UNIVERSITY OF MINNESOTA

ESSAYS TO MY
DAUGHTER

Other Books by Steven Simpson

THE LEADER WHO IS HARDLY KNOWN
The Art of Self-Less Teaching in the Chinese Tradition

THE PROCESSING PINNACLE
An Educator's Guide to Better Processing
(with Dan Miller and Buzz Bocher)

THE CHIJI GUIDEBOOK
A Collection of Experiential Activities and Ideas for Using Chiji Cards
(with Chris Cavert)

REDISCOVERING DEWEY
A Reflection on Independent Thinking

ESSAYS TO MY DAUGHTER

DAUGHTER

on Our Relationship With the Natural World

STEVEN SIMPSON

Purdue University Press • West Lafayette, Indiana

Copyright 2023 by Purdue University. All rights reserved.
Printed in the United States of America.

Cataloging-in-Publication Data is available from the Library of Congress.

978-1-61249-783-9 (paperback)
978-1-61249-784-6 (epub)
978-1-61249-785-3 (epdf)

The cover photo was taken from the dock of my cousin Tom McEwen's small lakeside resort in Hazelhurst, Wisconsin. Tom and I fished together as kids, and my family stayed at his resort when Clare was growing up. Clare learned to ride a bike there. Tom died only months before this book was published. The book's content is dedicated to Clare and her mom; the cover is for my cousin.

To Clare and Manyu

Contents

Preface

MY DAUGHTER, CLARE, WAS ASKED TO READ ONE NONFICTION BOOK over the summer before starting her junior year of high school. The list of approved books included *A Sand County Almanac*. When she asked for my recommendation as to which book to read, I was sitting at a table near my bookcase. I didn't even have to get out of my chair to pull a copy of *Sand County* off the shelf. I told her I first read Aldo Leopold's environmental classic[1] when I was just a few years older than her and would be interested in her opinion.

Clare read the book and then told me it didn't offer much that was new to her. "Dad," she said, "I already know that it is stupid to shoot wolves just to have more deer. I already look up in the sky when geese fly over."

My daughter may not have been the best person to ask whether *A Sand County Almanac* had anything to offer her generation. Maybe the reason for her tepid review really was because the book was beginning to show its age, but more likely it was because I'd been passing off Leopoldian ideas as my own for so long that Clare had already been exposed to much of what was in the book.

My own introduction to *A Sand County Almanac* came in college. My bachelor's degree is from the University of Wisconsin, the same school where Aldo Leopold taught and established the country's first game management program.[2] Leopold had been dead for twenty-five years when I showed up; still, his presence permeated the College of Agriculture side of campus. By the end of my sophomore year, I'd been assigned *A Sand County Almanac* as a reading in three different courses—a wildlife ecology course, an outdoor recreation course, and a landscape architecture course. If Wallace Stegner was correct in describing *A Sand County*

Almanac as "almost a holy book in conservation circles," I was on my way to becoming one of its disciples.[3] Even a clueless undergraduate in search of a major takes notice when the same book is required reading in multiple courses.

I still have the paperback copy of *A Sand County Almanac* from my undergraduate years.[4] The paper quality is barely better than newsprint. The pages now crumble if not handled carefully. I keep the book not out of nostalgia, but because there are forty-eight years of notes in the margins. If I discarded the book now, I would lose the most complete record of my personal environmental thinking.

Clare's reaction to *A Sand County Almanac* made me wonder whether my environmentalism was as stuck in the 1970s as my taste in music: Jackson Browne, Bruce Springsteen, Van Morrison, Aldo Leopold. Philosopher Kenn Maly once described *A Sand County Almanac* as the story of one man's transformation from traditional conservationist to biocentric preservationist.[5] If this interpretation is correct, a failure to progress beyond the insights of *A Sand County Almanac* might be missing the point. Environmental philosophies are supposed to evolve. They change. What if the land ethic as described in *A Sand County Almanac* was the culminating philosophy for Aldo Leopold, but meant to be a starting point for the rest of us?

To some extent, *Essays to My Daughter on Our Relationship with the Natural World* is a progress report on my philosophical growth since the first time I read *A Sand County Almanac*, but that is neither my motivation for the book nor its purpose. It began as a series of letters to Clare. She was about to head off for college, and our regular hikes and paddles together were about to come to an end. I envisioned a letter-writing campaign where I could periodically remind Clare of the role of nature in her life. It seemed to me a good idea at the time, but for two reasons, the letters never got sent. First of all, I had no reason to worry about my daughter. After she left for college, our telephone conversations often revolved around the new outdoor experiences she was having. Clare's connection to nature was firmly in place, and on matters of nature and the environment, she was more than capable of maintaining a connection on her own.

Secondly, the letters became more than simple reminders to my daughter. As often happens when someone takes the time to seriously write about an important subject, the content went off in unexpected directions. I intended to do no more than tell Clare to stay connected to the natural world, but I quickly found myself reflecting on how I'd introduced her to nature in the first place. The results, which I hope still maintain the intimacy of a conversation between a man and his daughter, touch on topics I believe will be of interest to a broader audience than just Clare. Stephen King once wrote that all of his books start out as letters to one person (in his case, to his wife, Tabitha),[6] and the same thing more or less happened here.

If you are an outdoorsperson who picked up this book, you probably are someone who already has a sense of his or her environmental ethic. If you are a parent who picked up this book, you likely are a mom or dad who already takes kids outdoors. In other words, you don't need an introductory lesson on humankind's relationship with the natural world. Still, I ask you to give the book a chance. It is a conscious effort to make informal environmental education and basic environmental philosophy accessible, pertinent, and personal without dumbing it down.[7]

Introduction

Personal Philosophy and Individual Experiences

IN A SEGMENT OF THE SHORT DOCUMENTARY *A PRIVATE UNIVERSE*,[1] Heather, a bright middle school student, is unable to explain how the earth revolves around the sun. Even after studying basic astronomy in school, her sketch of the earth's path is incorrect. Basically she has the earth flying past the sun, then making U-turns in outer space to keep from leaving the solar system. The point of the video clip is that the girl's confusion stemmed from having to reconcile two strong, but contradictory, sources of information. The first was a self-created image of the solar system that she'd informally pieced together over the years. The second was the astronomically correct pattern of the planets she'd learned in science class. When class content did not mesh with Heather's personal theories, she unconsciously blended old and new to come up with a convoluted model even she knew could not be right.

I mention Heather's story because I believe I created a similar situation with my college students when I taught the environmental philosophy portion of an Introduction to Environmental Studies course at the University of Wisconsin–La Crosse. Students came to my class with a homespun environmental philosophy based on their own experiences in nature. They usually had a hard time putting that philosophy into words, but it was there. When I tried to help them clarify their thinking by introducing them to deep ecology, social ecology, ecofeminism, and the land ethic of Aldo Leopold, I sometimes made things worse. The problem was not information overload so much as very practical conflicts between individual experience and course content. How, the students wanted to know, could they be a deep ecologist and still shoot a deer for sport? How could they look to technology for solutions when their gut said technology was part of the problem? How could they consider homo sapiens to be no different, no more important than mosquitoes and oak trees, but still think of themselves as stewards of the land?

One of the basic tenets of good teaching is to align new information with the students' knowledge base. When it came to teaching environmental philosophy, I somehow ignored this fundamental principle. I taught the subject as if the students were blank slates and had never thought about their relationship to nature. In retrospect, I wonder what I was thinking. My explicit goal was to help students comprehend, maybe advance, their environmental philosophies, yet I was teaching the subject of environmental philosophy as if their own experiences with the natural world were not at the heart of it all.

As readers will discover very early in this book, my work as an environmental educator followed two distinct tracks. One was the many hours I spent outdoors with my daughter. The other was the myriad of environmental studies and outdoor recreation courses I taught over a forty-year career. I am now retired, but if I was to return to the classroom, I'd flip my teaching strategy 180 degrees, start with the students' outdoor experiences, and, for the most part, not introduce academic philosophical concepts at all. I would, as I came to realize during the writing of this book, teach my students more in the way I taught my daughter. The majority of us don't need esoteric philosophical terminology to be good citizens of the earth. We need to understand for ourselves (and, at times, be able to convey to others) our personal relationship to the natural world.

❧ ❧ ❧

There are two basic ways to read this book. The first is to engage with it as a series of stand-alone personal essays. Each chapter has a story, and each story contains a simple commentary on humankind's relationship with nature. The chapters work as independent pieces of nature writing, and from that perspective, *Essays to My Daughter on Our Relationship with the Natural World* needs no introduction. I am not a big fan of introductory chapters in the first place, and I suggest anyone who is looking for light reading just before bed to skip this intro and go directly to the first essay.

If, however, someone is interested in using the book to better articulate his or her own environmental thinking or to teach others about nature, it will work best if I set the stage at least a little bit. I do not want to steer anyone's thinking in a particular direction, but neither do I want readers to sense a common thread running through the essays in this book, yet not be sure what the thread is. This is not a crime novel, and understanding the book's overall purpose from the get-go will do nothing to ruin the plot. If anything, frontloading the objectives should make the book more accessible and more enjoyable.

The purpose of this book is to point out that each individual has a personal environmental philosophy intertwined with his or her individual experiences in nature—but it takes a bit of conscious reflection to get it out. This observation may not seem like much of an insight to most outdoorsmen and outdoorswomen, but when I think back to the way I taught philosophy in my environmental studies course, I consider it a revelation.

The format of *Essays to My Daughter* follows that of *A Sand County Almanac*. Like Leopold's famous collection of essays, there are three main parts: two are nature-related stories and a third is a statement on environmental aesthetics. As a unit, the three parts are meant to be a broad prompt for readers to reflect on their own experiences in nature and, from those reflections, gain an understanding of how to pass their love of nature onto others.

Part I of this book, "The Pond and the Shack," describes personal experiences in nature that were enhanced by excerpts from traditional nature writing. Its purpose is to suggest it is not always enough to just spend time in the outdoors. We sometimes need help in interpreting nature's lessons, and one the best ways to do this is to turn to Aldo Leopold and his fellow nature writers for guidance. The Leopolds, Cathers, and Muirs of the world may not have experienced anything more spectacular than we have, but they expressed their thoughts about those experiences exceptionally well. I harped on my students to interact with nature firsthand, but that does not negate the need for great books.

Part II, "Sketches Here and There," is a collection of essays about place. At times, the chapters digress from direct experience in nature to contemporary issues in resource management and environmental education, but even then the predominant theme is the need to connect with nature wherever we are. Every place we live and every vacation spot we know well has something to teach us—and while it sounds like a cliché when I say it, each bioregion offers a unique perspective on the universality of humankind's relationship with nature.

All of the various events described in part II are unremarkable, which is the point. The stories are mine, and I have not, like Peter Matthiessen, scoured the Himalayas in search of the snow leopard. Neither have I, like Jane Goodall at the age of twenty-six, moved in with the chimpanzees. Part II is about commonplace occurrences that somehow affected my understanding of the natural world. They are about the kinds of moments most people have had or could easily have if they choose to, yet they still provide engaging experiences and valuable lessons.

Finally, part III, "Continuums," provides a basic vocabulary for articulating a personal environmental philosophy. It does this by looking at a variety of ways people perceive themselves in connection to nature. The first chapter asks *who* we are in terms of the fundamental delineation of conservation versus preservation. The next considers *why* we go to nature by focusing on the two motivations of challenge and a sense of peace. The third addresses *where* we find our connections to nature, and the fourth chapter is about *how* we best learn from her. A final chapter tries to put it all together by asking *what* it is we do to help nature along. If this does not quite make sense to you now, it will when you get there. The chapter titles in part III identify the various themes. They are

> The Preservationist and the Conservationist
> The Wanderer and the Adventurer
> The Homecomer and the Sojourner
> The Romantic and the Scientist
> The Restorer

Sometimes breaking down our relationship with nature and looking at its component parts can lead to problems. It may, for example, generate a laundry list of realizations rather than a holistic perspective. There are, however, benefits as well. One benefit is that a person is allowed to have viewpoints that, on the surface, seem contradictory. For example, a person can favor deer hunting, yet disapprove of an annual wolf hunt. He or she can see nature as a challenge to overcome and still want to be gently embraced by her. A person can be a libertarian generally opposed to big government and still be an ardent environmentalist. That last descriptor would have described my dad to a tee.[2] While he would have enjoyed the stories in this book, he also would have considered the overarching theme to be academic tripe from an overeducated son. And right there is another seeming inconsistency—a person can be a serious environmentalist and not give a lick about dissecting his or her environmental thinking.

Even though I trust readers to draw their own conclusions from the personal essays in this book, the educator in me cannot help but lay a little groundwork. Even John Dewey once stated that if teachers hold back *all* of their insights to allow students to learn entirely on their own, then the teachers' years of acquired knowledge serve no purpose.[3] From that perspective, I am going to ask readers to approach the chapters with the following three questions in mind:

1. What experiences in nature have you had that are every bit as interesting as the stories in this book, and what did you learn from those experiences?
2. What simple steps can you take to have more experiences like the ones you've already had?
3. What can you do with kids to get them started on their own meaningful experiences in the natural world?

These three questions provide a fairly good road map for basic nature-based environmental education. Each of us can spend time in nature, come to understand our relationship with the natural world, spend even more time in nature—and somewhere along the way, invite the next generation of outdoorspeople to tag along.

Part I

The Pond and the Shack

1

The Good Oak Redux

IF NOT FOR WALDEN POND, ALDO LEOPOLD'S SHACK WOULD BE THE
most iconic landmark in American environmental literature. Adjacent
to the Wisconsin River just outside the small city of Baraboo, Wisconsin, the abandoned chicken coop turned rustic cabin still stands and is
now the centerpiece of the Aldo Leopold Foundation. It is only a two-
hour drive from my home in La Crosse, so I frequently took students from
the University of Wisconsin–La Crosse for a visit. Although the education director at the foundation no longer allows it, she used to waive our
admission fee in exchange for a couple of hours of conservation work. The
work projects were a perfect arrangement. The foundation got its money's worth from our labor, my financially strapped department saved a
few dollars, and the students connected with the property in a way not
possible through a tour alone. Usually we pulled invasive garlic mustard. Twice we prepared prairie plots for prescribed burns. Once, on a
full-day outing, a handful of graduate students and I used drawknives to
shave the red pine logs that were going to be used in the construction of
the new interpretive center. The logs came from trees actually planted
by Leopold and his family. All of the students pocketed discarded strips
of pine bark from these trees and thought they'd come away with little
pieces of history.

Most of my students embody a strong Midwestern work ethic. They carry full class loads, have off-campus jobs, and often volunteer at places like the Boys and Girls Club or the local nature center. If they feel any sense of entitlement at all, it is because they consider college a privilege in itself. When we took on conservation projects at the Shack, the students worked hard for a full two hours, then to a person fell asleep during the van ride home. As the driver, I'd be caffeinated and the only one awake, and the silence gave me time to think back on the day.

On one of our drives back to La Crosse, I spent the whole trip thinking about Leopold's essay "The Good Oak." It was fresh in my mind because it had been highlighted on that year's tour. There is a plaque near the Shack that commemorates the spot where the actual Good Oak is thought to have stood. On all of my previous trips to the Leopold Foundation, there was no mention of the plaque. This year, our elderly docent not only took us to it, but had students stand in a circle around the little memorial and read aloud from the famous essay. None of the students had been to the Shack before, so they assumed the orchestrated reading was a standard part of the tour. I, having been on a dozen different tours with a dozen different guides, knew this not to be the case. The Good Oak, both the essay and the site, just happened to be this guide's personal penchant.

"The Good Oak" is the story of the Leopold family cutting down a tree that had been struck by lightning. In the process of sawing through the trunk with a two-person crosscut saw, Leopold reflected on the changes in Wisconsin's ecology during the life of the tree. As the saw blade dug into the successive rings of the tree's trunk, he recounted environmental events coinciding with the years those rings had been added to the tree's girth. Leopold presented his brief environmental history of Wisconsin in reverse chronological order, because the saw's sharp teeth cut into the most recent rings first. The deeper the cut, the older the rings.

Of the dozens of historical events listed by Leopold, the ones about extirpated species intrigue me the most. According to Leopold, martens disappeared from Wisconsin in 1925, cougars in 1908, turkeys in 1872, and elk in 1866. Except for the passenger pigeon (1899), all of the creatures Leopold categorized as gone are now back. Marten, turkey, and elk have been intentionally reintroduced. Mountain lions wandered in on their own.

The most remarkable return is that of the turkeys. I have never seen a marten or an elk or a cougar in Wisconsin, but it is nearly impossible these days to walk the edge of a wood lot without spooking a rafter of turkeys. For over eighty years beginning in the 1880s, conservation officers and private citizens had intermittently tried to reintroduce turkeys with no long-term success. All of these released birds, however, had been products of game farms and were either too domesticated or too dumb to survive and/or reproduce in a natural setting. Then in 1976, someone suggested introducing wild turkeys instead of tame ones, and the subsequent release of 363 birds has grown to a population of over 350,000.[1]

The return of the turkeys made me think about other environmental events that have happened in Wisconsin during my lifetime. All of them, of course, occurred decades after the writing of "The Good Oak." The list of invasive species would be a story unto itself. Along with garlic mustard, there would be purple loosestrife, gypsy moths, emerald ash borers, burdock, Canada thistle (a plant native to Eurasia in spite of its name), leafy spurge, honeysuckle, and more recently, Asian ladybugs and bighead carp. The most memorable invasive species for me is the alewife. As a kid growing up near Lake Michigan in the 1960s, summers meant a wide belt of dead herring at the high-water mark of every beach I ever played on. When I was eleven years old and at the peak of my lakeshore wanderings, alewife made up 90 percent of the fish mass in Lake Michigan.[2] Today the alewife population is greatly reduced, and the long ribbons of rotting alewife on the beach have been replaced by the equally ubiquitous remains of invasive zebra mussels. Mussel shells, however, don't stink, and I almost feel sorry for the current generation of young Great Lakes beachcombers. Decades from now, what foul aroma is going to remind these kids of the best part of their childhood?

At present, my outdoor play is not along Lake Michigan, but on Wisconsin's opposite natural border, the Mississippi River. Each spring the Upper Mississippi suffers a substantial winterkill. The backwaters are strewn with the decaying carcasses of carp, shad, and northern pike. Most fishermen avoid the smelliest areas, but I am drawn to them like a dog to roadkill. The smell of dead fish returns me to my childhood.

As I drove home from the Shack, other bits of nature-related state history came to mind. I list them here in reverse chronological order just as Leopold had, but I check them off according to the exits on Interstate 90 instead of tree rings. This carries with it a whole different connotation.[3]

EXIT 92   In 2014,[4] supervisors in Trempealeau County vote not to extend the moratorium on new sand quarries. Because Trempealeau County sand has consistent size and a high silica content, it is ideal for the hydraulic fracturing of oil and natural gas wells in North Dakota and other oil states. Exit 92 is the Interstate exit nearest the Shack.

EXIT 89   Also in 2014, Wisconsin's first case of white-nose syndrome is discovered in Grant County. The disease threatens to decimate the state's bat population. One of the main culprits for the spread of the disease are spelunkers who, unlike the bats, move from cave to cave.

EXIT 87   In 2010, after mining interests lose the legal battle over whether Indian reservations can set higher environmental standards than the federal government, the Ojibwe and Potawatomi Nations permanently protect a large tract of northeastern Wisconsin by using casino proceeds to buy the site of the proposed Crandon copper mine.

EXIT 85   In 2009, local police and a game warden shoot and kill a bear treed in La Crosse's Myrick Park. Near a popular playground, they do not wait for a tranquilizer gun to arrive. I was out of town that day, but a neighbor later told me the bear had wandered through my backyard before meeting its demise in the park.

EXIT 79   In 2005, all aquatic life in Jersey Valley Lake is killed by a run-off of liquid cow manure. Until then, Jersey Valley had been my favorite place to fish in the spring when the Mississippi River was running fast and the fish in the river were hard to find.

EXIT 69   In 1985, John Muir and Aldo Leopold are the first inductees into the Wisconsin Conservation Hall of Fame.

EXIT 61   In 1983, a historical marker commemorating Aldo Leopold is placed at the westbound I-90/94 rest stop near Mauston. The inscription on the marker opens with the quote, "There are some who can live without wild things, and some who cannot."

EXIT 55   In 1975, the Army Corps of Engineers abandons the La Farge Dam project on the Kickapoo River, but not before a hundred-plus landowners are forced off farms scheduled to be flooded by the proposed dam.

EXIT 48   In 1973, the International Crane Foundation is established just down the road from Aldo Leopold's Shack.

EXIT 45   Also in 1973, two Ojibwe fishermen intentionally stir the political pot by spearing walleye outside the Lac Courte Oreilles Indian Reservation. It sets off years of racial tension and legal battles as to whether old Indian treaties allow Native Americans to spearfish walleye on ceded territory. It is at Exit 45 that I-90 and I-94 split. I-90 veers due west toward La Crosse, and I-94 continues northwest to Eau Claire and the Twin Cities.

EXIT 43   In 1970, the Wisconsin legislature bans DDT. This is eight years after the publication of *Silent Spring,* but still two years before the pesticide is banned nationally.

EXIT 41   Also in 1970, through the efforts of Wisconsin senator Gaylord Nelson, the US celebrates the first Earth Day. I remember the event well. I was a sophomore in high school, and the entire student body left the school grounds to walk through the neighborhood west of campus. The parade route went right past my house, so my friends and I bailed to drink Cokes and eat potato chips at my kitchen table. As a kid I cared about the environment, but was too cynical to think that fifteen hundred indifferent high school kids marching around the block was going to make any difference.

EXIT 28   In 1968, the Wild and Scenic Rivers Act is passed. Wisconsin's St. Croix and Wolf Rivers are two of the eight waterways designated in the initial legislation.

EXIT 25   Also in 1968, environmentalists and other activists halt Project Sanguine. Sanguine was a plan to run six thousand miles of cable under twenty-two thousand square miles of land in northern Wisconsin. The project would have turned about a third of the state into a giant antenna. The antenna would have allowed the US Navy to communicate with submarines while the subs were underwater.

EXIT 15   In 1967, the Sparta-Elroy State Bicycle Trail becomes America's first rails-to-trails project. Rather than giving or selling the land from an abandoned railroad right-of-way to adjoining landowners, the berm is converted into a linear recreation corridor.

EXIT 12   In 1966, salmon are introduced into Lake Michigan. For years, these top predators were credited with controlling the alewife population. Recently, however, some biologists think a bigger reason for the alewife decline has been the appearance of plankton-syphoning zebra and quagga mussels.

EXIT 5   In 1958, the first section of Interstate highway in Wisconsin is completed. On some days, the sound of Interstate traffic can be heard from Leopold's Shack. Would Leopold have purchased the land had the Interstate System been in place at the time? The limited-access four-lane highway would have reduced travel time between his home in Madison and his rural retreat near Baraboo, but at what cost?

I left the Interstate at Exit 5, and some of the students woke up when they felt the van slowing down. I turned south onto Highway 16 and immediately drove past Pier 1, PetSmart, Old Navy, and a dozen chain restaurants. If not for the regionally based ShopKo and Farm & Fleet, we might have been on the outskirts of any town in America.[5] Once we got beyond the shopping hub, the roadway turned decidedly La Crosse. Directly to the east, sandstone bluffs towered over the four lanes of traffic. To the west, the La Crosse River Marsh paralleled the shoulder of the road. In the few spots where there was sufficient flat ground between the road and the bluffs or enough dry ground between the road and the river bottoms, local developers had squeezed in tiny strip malls.

Fifteen minutes later we reached campus. I parked outside the Health Sciences Center and the students piled out, some heading home and others to their part-time jobs. Before I pulled away from the curb to return the rental van, I jotted down as many of my recollections from the ride home as I could remember. Like Leopold's children, who have said they are not sure which one of the several oaks they cut down was the inspiration for their father's story, I didn't know whether this trip to the Shack would be distinguishable from any of the others.

As I put my thoughts to paper, I realized I'd just achieved what the National Park Service tries to accomplish in its interpretive programs.[6] I had personalized a historical site. Probably because I am from Wisconsin, I've always considered "The Good Oak" essay more than a collection of interesting factoids, but even so, the story always carried for me a sense of "that was then and this is now." By linking Leopold's old series of events to a more contemporary list of my own making, I'd bridged a gap between Leopold's story and mine. I'd made the Good Oak personally relevant. Now each time I reread *A Sand County Almanac* and come across the classic line, "Rest! cries the chief sawyer, and we pause for breath,"[7] I think not only about the Peshtigo Fire (1871) or the intentional introduction of carp (1879), but also about a bear in Myrick Park (2009) and my role in the first Earth Day (1970).

The Shack is the only place where the environmental history of the textbooks intersects with my personal geographic map. This strikes me as significant.

2

Drowning Out All Our Muskrats

WHEN I STEPPED DOWN FROM FULL-TIME WORK AFTER THIRTY YEARS
of college teaching, my colleagues at work threw me a small retirement
party. I should have known someone at the gathering was going to ask me
to say a few words, but I hadn't prepared anything beforehand. Someone
did ask, and with everybody waiting for me to thank the university for
many good years of meaningful employment, the first thing to pop into
my head was a story about floods and canoes and muskrats. Maybe the
story was waiting for the right time to come out . . .

🌿 🌿 🌿

I regularly took college students canoeing on the backwaters of the Upper
Mississippi River. The Mississippi River from Minneapolis to St. Louis,
which includes my section of the great waterway, is a series of pools created by a system of locks and dams.[1] Each pool has a dredged navigation
channel down the center, plus acres of shallow backwaters off to either
side. Commercial barges and most of the deep-hulled recreational boats
keep to the main channel, so paddling a canoe or kayak between the river's red and green navigation markers is the nautical equivalent of bicy-
cling on a four-lane highway. The waters outside the channel, however, are
relatively undisturbed and provide some of the best flatwater paddling in

the Midwest. When water levels are low, the backwaters offer meandering passageways through weedy marshlands. When water levels are high, the aquatic vegetation vanishes beneath the surface of the water, and the narrow corridors of the backwaters widen into a chain of long shallow lakes.

One particular spring the water levels were especially high. Rapid snow melt combined with heavy spring rains put the river at flood stage. Long sections of the river were designated no wake. All watercraft had to move slowly enough that their passing did not erode the adjacent riverbanks.

Motorboaters tend to stay off the water altogether during periods of no wake. So too do most canoeists and kayakers, but for nonmotorized watercraft, this is a mistake. So long as paddlers are safety conscious, April and early May can offer unique opportunities for solitude. I wanted to take my students onto the river during this time, but worried about the strength of the current. I kayaked the planned route two days before the class outing and determined the backwaters to be safe for first-time paddlers. The trip with my class was on.

It turned out to be a remarkable afternoon. Two dozen students and I put in at Goose Island just south of La Crosse. Under normal conditions, the island sits anywhere from two to twelve feet above the waterline. On the day we paddled, easily an eighth of the island was underwater. We could not put in at the usual boat landing, as it was totally submerged, but we found a gently sloping low spot adjacent to one of the park's picnic shelters. Students were able to paddle their boats over what should have been dry land, and they gently weaved their way through flooded trees. Maples, birches, box elders, and cottonwoods poked directly out of the river.[2] The water that day was like glass, and the trees had not yet leafed out. Even under normal conditions, a perfect reflection of trees on water can be mildly disorienting. That day, with bare trees standing in the water and my students paddling among them, the view was surreal.

This otherworldly riverscape, however, was not even the highlight of the trip. The marshlands of the Upper Mississippi River are prime habitat for muskrats. A consequence of the high water was that the muskrats' domed lodges were flooded. Usually the interiors of the rats' homes are well above the waterline. Muskrats build lodges with the entrances below the surface, but everything else, including their cozy living quarters, are designed to be high and dry. On this day, the living quarters were underwater, and only the very tops of the lodges poked up out of the river.

As we canoed past the exposed peaks of the muskrat lodges, each dome had one or two muskrats curled up on top. With their usual daytime chambers flooded, the aquatic mammals had nowhere else to go. On a typical midday outing, I see four or five muskrats. That spring afternoon the students and I saw over a hundred.

Sleeping on top of their lodges is not a prudent practice for muskrats. Eagles are a predator of the aquatic rodents, and napping in the open makes them easy prey. Fortunately for the rats, spring floods also bring winterkill. Bloated fish carcasses so littered the backwater that the less experienced paddlers in class repeatedly bumped into them with their boats. Eagles, despite their reputation as hunters, are scavengers at heart and prefer dead fish over live and feisty muskrats.

Paddling among the muskrats reminded me of a Henry David Thoreau quote that had never made any sense to me. In *Walden*, he had written, "Even this may be the eventful year, which will drown out all our muskrats." I'd never understood how muskrats could be drowned out, but now I'd witnessed it for myself.

That only meant, however, that I understood "drowning out muskrats" in literal terms. Thoreau intended it as a metaphor—and metaphorically, I was still at a loss. That evening, back at home, I sat in my favorite chair with a blanket over my legs and opened a copy of *Walden*. The section about drowning out muskrats appears in the final pages of the book. The complete quote is

> The life in us is like the water in the river. It may rise this year higher than man has ever known it, and flood the parched upland; even this may be the eventful year, which will drown out all our muskrats.[3]

Immediately after this quote, Thoreau told a story about an insect larva that, after more than sixty years of dormancy within the wood of an old table, gnaws its way out and emerges as a "strong and beautiful bug." I interpret Thoreau's words as a wake-up call telling me to work past any obstacles and live the life I was meant to live.

That's my retirement story and the lesson that goes with it. Until I told it to a small group of colleagues, I didn't even know I had a retirement story. Stephen Jay Gould once wrote that three elements tend to be in place for a person to come up with a fresh idea.[4] The first two occur in no particular order or, perhaps more accurately, occur continuously and interchangeably. They are (1) the person has a variety of experiences and (2) the person reads. Gould was adamant that the experiences and the readings be broad and extend beyond the person's usual areas of expertise. The third element is (3) a bit of luck. Gould went on to state he preferred this arbitrary and somewhat mundane method for original thinking to its alternative, the eureka moment. Eureka moments or flashes of genius, according to Gould, are limited to . . . well, limited to geniuses, which means the rest of us can only sit around and wait for guys like Einstein and Darwin to do our thinking for us. Conversely, seeking out experiences, reading broadly, and being ready when fortuitous opportunities present themselves is something that all of us can do. None of us are likely to come up with anything as groundbreaking as relativity or evolution, but all of us can formulate ideas that are new to us.

As far as I can tell, my muskrat story closely adheres to Gould's formula. Had I only read *Walden* and not gone canoeing with my students, there would be no story. Had I only gone canoeing and never read *Walden*, I would not have attached meaning to the flooded muskrat lodges. Had I not been caught unprepared at my own retirement party, the story would not have emerged like an insect from an old tabletop. Only because I'd read nature writing *and* experienced nature firsthand *and* extemporaneously recounted the events on the river to my coworkers did the timely lesson coincide with my retirement. Yet here it was.

As careers go, college teaching affords more autonomy than most, but like all jobs, I spent a part of each day working on tasks that were not intrinsically rewarding. Upon retirement, these boring job-related responsibilities got passed on to a very competent colleague who agreed to take over my administrative duties. My newfound freedom happened quickly, but at the time of the retirement party had not yet sunk in. Still, I got the point of my own story right away. I suspect Thoreau would have admonished me for waiting so long to take full responsibility for my life, but the very point of the muskrat metaphor is that it is never too late to find a new path.

Of course, eliminating old tasks is only a first step. The real measure of a change in life is the extent to which we replace old routines with new and interesting pursuits. For me, writing for pleasure is one of those new activities, so finally putting this story to paper has been a good start. My retirement story is already pointing me in the right direction.

3

Wild Apples

ONE SUMMER MANY YEARS AGO I SPENT TWO MONTHS RUNNING A CAMP counselor training program adjacent the redwoods in Northern California. For eight consecutive one-week sessions, co-instructor Chris Schmidt and I camped out with a small group of high school students and taught them basic skills for working with young kids in a natural setting. My favorite activity of the week was a hike that concluded in an abandoned apple orchard not far from our campsite. In the heart of the orchard stood a big maple tree. Maple trees located deep in the forest tend to grow tall and straight as they compete with other trees for sunlight. This maple grew in a clearing with a scattering of old, short apple trees. Sunlight was plentiful, and the maple did not concentrate all of its energy growing skyward. Instead, it grew outward like a burr oak in a Midwestern oak savanna. Although I did not know it at the time, the tree was so distinctive that it appeared on the cover of an album by guitarist William Ackerman.[1] My interest in the tree was that it was broad enough for me and a dozen high school students to easily climb into its lower limbs and find comfortable resting spots.

I would ask each student to pick an apple from one of the nearby apple trees before climbing into the maple. Then, once everyone had squirmed into a nook among the branches, I read excerpts from Thoreau's *Wild*

Apples. When I got to the part where Thoreau encounters his own abandoned apple orchard and bites into an apple he claims has been "sea-
soned" by its wildness, I asked the students to taste their own apples.
Our apples, while still very green, were, to my taste, pleasantly tart. My
mom would have described them as good pie apples. After the students
gave their apples a try, I offered them the choice of finishing their apples
or tossing them aside. Always some students kept eating; always some
students did not.

In the essay, Thoreau goes on to say he would fill his pockets with fruit
from the wild apple trees and take it home—only to discover that the apples delicious on the trail were, when eaten at home, "sour enough to set
a squirrel's teeth on edge." He concludes that apples from abandoned apple orchards are like nature writing and best consumed outdoors:

> I would have my thoughts, like wild apples, to be food for walkers, and
> will not warrant them to be palatable, if tasted in the house.[2]

Here is one of the few instances where I disagree with Thoreau. It is
romantic to think nature writing is best read in the wild, but that has not
been my experience. As far as my own outings go, how many times have
I carried *The Singing Wilderness* or *Desert Solitaire* into the backcountry
and never taken it out of my pack? Once in the wild, there are better ways
to spend daylight hours than by reading. At night I prefer a small fire, one
too small to shed enough light for easy reading. Just before falling asleep,
reading a few pages from inside my sleeping bag does nicely cap off a long
day, but I carry only the bare essentials with me on my trips. The pleasure
of reading myself to sleep is offset by the worry that I am sucking the life
out of my only set of flashlight batteries. As a result, I seldom read outdoors, and reciting *Wild Apples* from the branches of that maple tree was
more the exception than the rule.

I've read several authors who celebrate the reading of books "outside
the enclosure of walls, where their pages get dirty and have to be held
down against the whipping of the wind,"[3] but I've encountered no one

who has written about *not* reading books in nature. It may not be anything worth mentioning, even though I am doing so now.

When I read nature writing, it usually is from a comfortable chair with a glass of Wild Turkey in my hand. The smallest thimble of bourbon suffices as I seldom drink it. Mostly I just hold the liquor under my nose and let the peaty aroma serve as a substitute for the fireplace I don't have. I usually sit in the chair next to my living room's large front window—which makes no logical sense because I do most of my reading at night, and the view from the window is nothing more than dark silhouettes of a few trees and my neighbor's pickup truck. Even that view is lost the instant I turn on my reading lamp, because all I see then is my own reflection in the window glass.

I sometimes read nature writing about places I might someday go, but I most enjoy essays about the places I have already been. I read Sigurd Olson only after I paddled the Boundary Waters, read very little John Muir before I backpacked Yosemite, and had never picked up *Life on the Mississippi* until I moved, at the age of thirty-nine, to a river town upstream of Mark Twain's old stomping grounds. In each case, *re*visiting a place through the eyes of a good writer enhanced all that I'd learned on my own. I had read *Walden* one time before my initial pilgrimage to Concord, but it was for an undergraduate lit course. Only after wading thigh deep into the waters of Walden Pond on my own did I delve into the book without it being assigned. Not surprisingly, it made infinitely more sense the second time around.

I sometimes wonder if reading *Wild Apples* ever made a lasting impression on any of the students who sat with me in the abandoned apple orchard. It is the one thing I most remember from the summer of '82, and while *Wild Apples* is not one of Thoreau's most heralded short essays, it remains my favorite.

4

Still Fishing

FOR ME, ONE OF HENRY DAVID THOREAU'S MOST EVOCATIVE STATE-
ments was his response to friends who wondered whether their kids
should be allowed to hunt and fish. He wrote:

> Such [hunting and fishing] is oftenest the young man's introduction
> to the forest and the most original part of himself. He goes thither at
> first as a hunter and fisher, until at last, if he has the seeds of a better
> life in him, he distinguishes his proper objects, as a poet or naturalist
> it may be, and leaves the gun and fish-pole behind.[1]

I enjoy every word of this passage, but am most drawn to the part
where I've fallen short. Fishing during childhood unquestionably paved
the way for my adult career as a naturalist, but I have yet to "distinguish
[my] proper objects" and leave the fish pole behind. I continue to derive as much pleasure from fishing now as I ever have—and at the age of
sixty-eight (and unexpectedly set in my ways), I don't foresee my love
of fishing ever going away.

Thoreau himself continued to fish throughout his life, but wrote that
it diminished him a little bit each time he went out. He enjoyed fishing

and ate fish with his limited red meat diet, but he also questioned taking the life of an animal that had as much right to live as he did.[2] I appreciate Thoreau's misgivings on an intellectual level, but have yet to feel them in my bones.

I like to fish as an adult, and in some ways, I shouldn't make more of it than that. The only obvious differences between fishing as a kid and fishing as an adult are the composition of my gear and the need for solitude. As a ten-year-old, I fished with my dad's hand-me-down pole, a jackknife, a bait box, and an aspirin bottle of spare hooks and split shot. The only piece of equipment not absolutely necessary was my metal stringer. While I needed something for bringing fish back to camp, a short hank of twine would have worked almost as well.[3] The only upgrade I ever wanted in my gear was a different rod. Mine was one solid pole. It did not break down into two sections. This worked fine when I traveled by car with my dad, but the pole was too long to fit across my handlebars when I went off on my bicycle.

I am sure I over-romanticize the carefree nature of fishing as a boy. Still, when I compare today's gadgetry to the barebones angling of my childhood, the latter approach strikes me as the more intimate. There is a Thoreau quote for most nature-related topics, and when it comes to fishing, the phrase that comes to mind is, "Simplify, simplify."[4]

That is not to say I am immune to newfangled fishing gear. My current rods and reels cost hundreds of dollars, and my canoe is made of high-end Kevlar. A good canoe, however, is essential. Easy access to the Mississippi River backwaters increases my solitude as much as it does my catch. And while I have never owned a motorboat, I rarely turn down an invitation to join friends who are going out on theirs. Of all of the features on tricked-out fishing boats, I like depth finders the best.[5] When my friends slowly troll over the same spots I sometimes paddle in my canoe, I carefully study the contours of the river bottom. I watch for depressions and knolls, learning more about the underwater topography from the boat's sonar than I ever could from repeatedly lowering a small weight over the gunwales of my canoe.

When I am in my canoe or my kayak, the Mississippi River really only comes in two depths. Usually the river is either deeper than a normal paddle stroke or it isn't. On the rare occasions when I unintentionally capsize my boat, the pertinent unit of measure changes from the length of my paddle blade to the length of my body. The exact dimensions of the river instantly take on greater significance, and I develop a newfound interest in both water depth and the distance to shore. Nineteenth-century steamboat pilot Samuel Clemens measured his river by counting knots in a weighted rope. When I flip my boat, I use a more personal yardstick, that being the distance from my tiptoes to my chin.

My family never owned a boat, so as a young boy I fished from shore. Today, other than trout fishing, the only time I fish from shore is when I fish with kids. I fished from shore with my daughter, Clare, when she was young, and I now do the same with nieces and nephews and with the grandchildren of friends. Helping children with tangled lines and misdirected casts is impossible from a canoe. From shore, the task remains a full-time job, but is manageable. Furthermore, fishing from shore gives bored fisherboys and fishergirls the freedom to wander. When there is no action on the bobbers, they can chase frogs, wade in the shallows, and throw stones even if it spooks the fish. For a child, a slow day of fishing from a boat lasts about an hour. From shore, a slow day lasts as long as the adult in charge lets it go. One of my favorite things to do when kids wander away from our fishing spot is to catch a fish on my pole, discreetly re-hook it onto one of the kids' lines, and then call the kids over to reel it in. I doubt the fish thinks much of this practice, but I learned long ago that getting children excited about nature sometimes comes with an environmental impact.

But I am avoiding the main question. Why do I continue to fish? Why haven't I matured to the point where I can derive just as much pleasure from nature without harassing one of her creatures? At least as far back as The Compleat Angler,[6] serious fishermen have reflected on the allure of fishing. I have read some of this literature, and the stated reasons, as often as not, do not apply to me. I do not derive a particular sense of accomplishment by procuring my own dinner. I don't go after trophy fish and wouldn't know how to handle a big northern pike or massive catfish if I ever brought one alongside my canoe. I do see how fishing touches an innate need for independence, but here I have actually matured a little bit. For me, wilderness camping satisfies that particular yearning more than fishing does.

I have come up with four reasons why I have not outgrown the desire to fish. For all four, "have not outgrown" is the right way to phrase it. In each case, I see where I have failed to reach a higher plane in my relationship with the natural world. The zen of fishing is to not fish at all, and I am not yet there.

1. I fish for the peace and quiet.

I often fished alone as a kid, but I do not remember ever intentionally seeking out solitude. Now the chance to be alone is probably the No. 1 reason for going out at all. If I have not fully matured as a naturalist, it is because I have not developed the ability to do nothing in nature for long periods of time. Fishing, even when it is little more than waiting for a twitch in the line, is a form of action. If I sit quietly in a backwater without a pole, I am entertained for fifteen, maybe twenty minutes. Then I become bored. If I am in the same backwater with a pole in my hands, I can remain in the very same spot, watch the birds, listen to the sounds of nature, never get a bite, and still be engaged until impending darkness forces me off the water.

2. I feel like a kid when I fish.

Even if Thoreau hoped I might grow up and put childhood pastimes behind me, one of the appeals of fishing is that it is a socially acceptable way to remain childlike. Other than reading for pleasure and watching movies, fishing may be the only adult leisure pursuit to overlap with the fun things I did as a boy. Furthermore, living on the Mississippi River adds a second dimension to my childish behavior. Not only do I get to relive my own childhood when I fish this particular body of water, but I get to experience Huckleberry Finn's. Who doesn't want to be a little bit more like the freest spirit in all of American literature?

3. *Fishing connects me to nature in a way that other forms of outdoor recreation do not.*

It is not possible for me to completely explain the appeal of fishing, because I don't understand it all myself. What should I call the bond I feel when I observe an osprey take a fish at the same time I am trying to do the same?

4. *Fishing remains fun.*

Having fun may trump the other three reasons on this list. I continue to enjoy the challenge of reading water and discovering a good fishing hole on a previously unexplored stretch of river. I still value the thrill of a strike on an artificial lure, the study of fish ecology to learn the seasonal movements of a specific species of fish, and the novelty of catching a walleye, a northern pike, and a smallmouth bass all on the same day.

As I compile these reasons for fishing, I realize I really do not care why I fish any more than I care why I write nature essays or read detective novels. The best hobbies do not ask for justification. If anything, fishing has become a bigger part of my life than it's ever been, in part because some of my other outdoor pursuits have fallen by the wayside. I no longer backpack because of bad knees. I no longer rock climb because I've grown to accept my own mortality (i.e., I've stopped doing things that scare me too much). I used to do a little nature photography, but was not so enamored with that pastime that I bothered to reoutfit myself when all of the equipment went digital. I have abandoned several of my younger man outdoor pursuits, but the total time I spend in nature remains the same. That means either finding new activities in the outdoors or spending more time with the ones I have left. I don't see myself taking up watercolors, windsurfing, or car camping in overcrowded state parks, so I fish.

5

A Person's Leisure Time

I HAVE BEEN CRITICIZED FOR OVERANALYZING MY LEISURE. AFTER thirty years of teaching leisure theory in various college-level courses, I cannot help but turn some of the academic mumbo jumbo back on myself. Former students would call it karma.

One example of this overanalysis is a compulsion to categorize the use of my discretionary time. In general, I have three designations. Category one is *wasting time*. These are activities that entertain me, but have little or no intrinsic value. For example, I read too much popular fiction and follow the Green Bay Packers too closely. With the advent of streaming, I also watch too much television. I do not chastise myself for engaging in mindless diversion, because there is nothing wrong with it. Wasting time is not bad; it's just not constructive, nor is it contemplative.

Category two is *voluntary obligations*. Community service is the best example of this, but it also included helping my daughter with her homework when she was in grade school and, if I go back far enough, helping my Taiwanese wife with her English when we first moved to the US from Taiwan. This is an important category, because it usually takes precedence over other free time activities. I can't say I spend too much time on voluntary obligations, because I don't know how much is too much—but, for many, the commitment sometimes gets to the point where it feels like a burden. There is obligation and there is burden, and leisure, even in service to others, should not be burdensome.

The final category is true *leisure*. Many would say that watching TV and following the Packers qualify as leisure, but I disagree. Leisure has an important component not present in diversionary activities, and it is this:

> Participation in true leisure pursuits
> contributes to a life lived well.

This loftier notion of leisure dates back to Aristotle. He believed leisure to be the basis of culture and the path to happiness. Such a perspective significantly narrows the activities that qualify. Aristotelian leisure includes art, music, physical activity for a healthy body, politics in the form of service to the general populace, and above all, contemplation. According to Aristotle, contemplation is what most sets humanity apart from other living creatures—and, therefore, is the most worthwhile thing we can do with our lives.[1] Philosophy is a form of contemplation, but so is the reading of serious literature, prayer, and engagement in intelligent conversation. Spending quiet time in nature is contemplative leisure.

The term "leisure class" sometimes conjures up images of conspicuous consumption and jet-setting junkets to exclusive tourist destinations.[2] This is the antithesis of Aristotelian leisure. Serious practitioners of contemplative leisure tend not to care about wealth. Earning discretionary income to afford frivolous recreation takes time away from true leisure, and spending money on self-indulgent pleasures runs contrary to reflective endeavors. Aristotle claimed men [and women][3] of true leisure would be perceived by society as odd, because they valued free time more than riches. They rejected the luxuries that excessive discretionary income afforded.[4] Men and women of true leisure need enough money to not have to worry about satisfying basic needs, but live lives of moderation and simplicity.

One element of Aristotelian leisure that perhaps differs the most from more common definitions of the word is that nothing in the Aristotelian definition of leisure mentions fun. Fun is not prohibited. It is simply irrelevant, in part because fun is not considered a prerequisite to personal fulfillment.

While fun might not have been important to Aristotle, it is to me. I seek out leisure activities that are both contemplative and fun. Creative writing falls into that sweet spot. So does spending time in nature, which probably explains why just about every nature writer I've ever read eventually comes around to writing about recreation and leisure from a contemplative perspective. For example:

Aldo Leopold: "The man who cannot enjoy his leisure is ignorant, though his degrees exhaust the alphabet, and the man who does enjoy his leisure is to some extent educated, though he has never seen the inside of a school."[5]

John Muir, in reference to compulsory education: "Why not add compulsory recreation? ... Few think of pure rest or of the healing power of nature."[6]

Henry David Thoreau: "It would be glorious to see mankind at leisure for once. It is nothing but work, work, work. ... I think that there is nothing, not even crime, more opposed to poetry, to philosophy, ay, to life itself, than this incessant business."[7]

When I was in graduate school, two friends and I skipped class to go rock climbing at Taylors Falls along the St. Croix River on the Minnesota–Wisconsin border. There is a paved walking trail running directly behind the place where the belayers usually set up. Maurice was climbing, George was belaying, and I was backing up George on the belay. An old man, probably no older than I am now, walked up to us and asked, "What do you young fellas do for a living that you don't have to be at work today?"

"We're students," I answered.

The old man asked, "So what are you studying?"

"This," I said, pointing toward Maurice on the rock with my fist without letting go of the rope. "We are studying recreation."

"Yeah," said George. "And we're getting PhDs in it, too."

The old man replied, "Cripes, now I've heard everything," and he walked away in disgust.

If only more people saw nature-related leisure as time well spent or a discipline worth studying. Instead they, or should I say we as a society, associate time in nature with recreation and play—and then define recreation and play as idleness and diversion. So long as leisure pursuits are seen as taking us away from what we consider more important tasks, they will never be fully appreciated.

Richard Louv, the author of *Last Child in the Woods*, went so far as to ask environmental educators not to link their programs to play, recreation, or leisure. He felt any association between environmental education and recreation diminished environmental education's worth in some people's eyes. Instead Louv recommended that fun activities in nature be called "an essential investment in our children's health."[8] When I first read this, I am not sure which bothered me more, his logic or his wordiness, but I wanted to scream, "Why not just teach people the true value of leisure?" Unfortunately my own efforts to teach the true value of leisure have met with mixed results, so I see the rationale of Louv's end around.

Journalist Tiziano Terzani captured this commonly held low opinion of leisure in his book *A Fortune-Teller Told Me*.[9] The book is a memoir of Terzani's travels through Asia by train, boat, and bus. A Hong Kong fortune-teller had told him not to board a plane for a year, and to Terzani's own surprise, he heeded the warning. While in Indonesia, Terzani lamented that the country was developing economically, but a disproportionate amount of the money was going into the pockets of Chinese expatriates and not to native residents. He speculated the reason for this was because the average Indonesian only worked hard enough to afford basic needs, whereas many of the Chinese who emigrated to Indonesia went there specifically to get rich. Terzani made his point with an analogy of two fishermen in the same village, one Indonesian and one Chinese.

The Indonesian fisherman fills his boat with fish in just half a day, so after bringing in his catch around noon, he celebrates by relaxing, enjoying a beer, and spending the afternoon with his family. The Chinese fisherman also has a successful morning on the water, so right after bringing in his catch, he heads back out to sea to catch more fish. The Chinese fishermen is perceived as industrious, the Indonesian as somewhat lazy.[10]

On a professional level, I like Terzani's story because it personifies succinctly two opposing attitudes toward work and leisure. On a personal level, I am drawn to it because the activity Terzani used to represent hard work is the same activity I consider a favorite leisure pursuit. What am I to make of that?

6

Book Purge

DURING THE COVID-19 PANDEMIC, POLITICAL PUNDITS CONTINUED TO
appear on television, but did so from their homes rather than from their
studios. As often as not, bookshelves were used as a backdrop, and it became a popular pastime of viewers to scan the shelves of these talking
heads to see what books they possessed. For appearances' sake, I assume
that prior to their first telecast from home, all of these TV personalities or
their media consultants rearranged titles, straightened spines, and dusted
off volumes that hadn't been touched in years.

I will not be preparing my bookshelves for any upcoming televised appearances, but I remember well the last time I gave my personal library a
major overhaul. It was five years ago just prior to my retirement. During
my last several years at the University of Wisconsin–La Crosse, I had two
offices on campus. One was my department office for teaching, and the
other was an office in Main Hall from which I carried out a number of
administrative duties. With bookshelves at home and bookcases in two
different places at the university, I had a home library, a work library, and
an annex to my work library. During that time, I doubt I discarded a single book that came my way.

This hoarding of books made reducing my collection just prior to
retirement a formidable task. Over a period of a few months, I had

to condense three libraries into one. I held in my hands every book I owned and, in each instance, decided its fate. For the first time in a quarter century, I was forced to seriously decide which books I treasured, which wasted space, and which, while not necessarily among my favorites, met the vague threshold for being kept. My wife, Manyu, made it clear I could only have as many books in the house as fit on my share of our home's bookcases and built-in bookshelves. I'd be allowed to stack a few additional books on my bedside table, but I wasn't going to have books boxed in the basement or piled on the floor alongside my recliner. I lobbied for more space by pointing out that the best indicator of whether children read is the presence of books in the home—but even I recognized this as a weak argument. Our only daughter had just graduated from high school and was about to leave for college. Neither Manyu nor I believed a sudden influx of books was going to change Clare's reading habits.

My book purge consisted of two separate phases, one surprisingly easy and the other fairly hard. The easy part was going through the books that were already in the house. At home I had shelves of popular fiction, mostly crime novels, and had only to rid myself of the ones I'd already read once and knew I would never read again. If I did not attach particular significance to a particular title, it was gone. James Patterson and John Sandford took big hits. Early Robert B. Parker survived the culling; his later stuff did not.

The difficult part was at work, where I needed to decide which books were so indispensable that they got to come home. Textbooks were the first to be discarded. Many of them were complimentary copies from publishers and had barely been cracked. Their disposal reminded me of a colleague who'd once told me we needed the word "textbook" in our vocabulary to differentiate textbooks from real books. Next came the non-textbooks about current issues in outdoor recreation and environmental education. I knew I no longer needed these volumes for my work, but passing them on to colleagues was a deliberate statement that I was really stepping away from my life as a professor. Finally I had to go through the books on nature writing, philosophy, and ecology to determine which ones would make the final cut. One part of me said to keep them all. Another part said to find within me the twenty-two-year-old kid who used to throw his backpacking gear, a duffel bag of clothes, and a half dozen books in the back of an old Vega and then, without a second thought, leave everything else on the curb.

Several of the books were as easy to keep as others had been to discard, and the easiest to keep were those from my books-everyone-ought-to-read-before-they-die collection. The idea for this particular group of books came out of a graduate course I took from a professor named Harvey Sarles nearly forty years ago. Sarles is the closest I've come to studying alongside a Renaissance man. The name of his course was Pedagogy of Higher Education, but class discussions wandered into philosophy, literature, linguistics, ecology, human geography, anthropology, sociology, and psych. Sarles had no required readings, but once every class meeting he would write a title of a book on the pre-whiteboard chalkboard, then declare it a book to be read sometime in our lives. "Plato's *Republic*," he would say. "You need to read *The Republic* before you die." "*Crime and Punishment*. You should read this book when the time is right."

He explained that great books should not be assigned. They had to be read only when a person was ready for them. He once stood up and stated, "Kenneth Boulding's *The Image*. I think you should read it sometime before you die." I was interested enough in his brief description of the book that I immediately went out and bought it. Two weeks later, I spoke up in class. "I read *The Image*, but I don't think I understand it." Sarles asked me what I thought the book was about, and after I gave my answer, he said, "You are right. You don't understand it."

And that was the extent of his response. He went on to a completely different subject. I was stunned, and I think the rest of the small class of six PhD students was just as surprised. A few class meetings later, however, Sarles circled back to my reading of the book and said, "I was abrupt with Steve last week when he asked about *The Image*. I need to explain myself. I could have interpreted Boulding's book for him, but that would have served no purpose. Steve is not ready for *The Image*. If I explain the book to him now, he will put the book aside forever. If I don't explain it to him now, his lack of understanding will gnaw at him and he will read it again in a year or two. Then he will figure it out for himself."

I did read the book a year later, and it did make more sense.[1] More significantly, the events surrounding *The Image* led me to start my own list of books I'd like all of my students to read sometime before they die. Not surprisingly, *The Image* was inducted into the collection, but not before *A Sand County Almanac* and *Walden*. Over the years, I've come up with a few more titles. Now there are thirteen books on the list, but they take up double space on my shelves. I always keep two copies of each—a loaner copy that I hope does not come back when I loan it out and a noncirculating copy that was my own introduction to the book. The books are

> *A Sand County Almanac* by Aldo Leopold
> *Walden* by Henry David Thoreau
> *The Image* by Kenneth Boulding
> *Democracy and Education* by John Dewey
> *Tao Te Ching* by Laotze
> *Interpreting Our Heritage* by Freeman Tilden
> *The Importance of Living* by Lin Yutang
> *O Pioneers!* by Willa Cather
> *Leisure: The Basis of Culture* by Josef Pieper
> *Pedagogy of the Oppressed* by Paulo Freire
> *Mountains Without Handrails* by Joseph Sax
> *The Essays of Ralph Waldo Emerson*
> *Civil Disobedience* by Henry David Thoreau

The only book I would consider taking off the list is Emerson's *Essays*, and that's only because I don't yet understand it myself. I sense that, more than any other author, Emerson is going to teach me something really important once I am ready to read him. Now in retirement and collecting Social Security, I am beginning to wonder whether that day will ever come.

I've never put these titles in a written list before, mostly because every time I've ever shown my special collection to friends, they immediately point out its shortcomings. Even if they ignore my bias toward outdoor recreation, which almost no one ever does, they tell me the list is too American or too white or too heavy with the transcendentalists. Women, but not so much men, notice that if not for *O Pioneers!*, I'd have no women authors and no fiction.[2] One person asked me why all of the authors were dead. Had I stopped reading good books after I turned forty?[3]

I was not surprised to discover my read-before-you-die list was a representative sample of the kinds of books to make the final cut in my attempts to pare down my office libraries. The books I boxed to bring home were not unlike the read-before-you-die collection, a combination of nature writing, leisure theory, and a sampling of Eastern and Western philosophy. The only books to get boxed that did not have a comparable title on the before-you-die list were my plant and animal identification guides.

In the end, twelve boxes of books made their way to my house. To make room for them, ten boxes at home were set aside for the next church book sale. I brought home more books than I cleared space for, but I'd made a good faith effort to reduce the size of my overall library. Between work and home, I gave away nearly half of the books I'd accumulated during my years in La Crosse.

As I unpacked the boxes from work and tried to fit Dillard, McPhee, Lopez, and the *Peterson Guide to Eastern Birds* onto newly created shelf space, I couldn't help but wonder what these books had contributed to my own environmental thinking. My first realization was that, with the exception of *Silent Spring*, there were no volumes about specific environmental issues. There was nothing about climate change or wind turbines or mercury in fish. All of those books had been given away back at the university. The books to survive the cut were about personal accounts of time in nature. This was revealing, as it demonstrated that my reading coincides with my attitude toward the natural world. I occasionally advocate for environmental causes out of a sense of duty, but my overwhelming preference is to be a hermit-like naturalist.

Truth be told, environmental activists sometimes wear me out. Like many passionate politicos, they tend to be self-righteous. Joseph Sax observed in *Mountains Without Handrails* that environmentalists are elitists who serve an important purpose. They are a privileged minority who think they know better than everyone else about what humankind needs in regard to the nonhuman world and therefore push a particular agenda and achieve results that belie their numbers.[4] While they fully realize their successes are "many victories in a losing war,"[5] they remain determined to save people from themselves. I have friends and acquaintances whose self-worth is tied to their environmental activism, and I am forever grateful to these people for fighting the good fight more persistently and more effectively than I ever have.

Mountains Without Handrails is on my read-before-you-die-list, but not for its commentary on environmental politics. It's there because it promotes what Sax called reflective recreation. Reflective recreation essentially is nature-based, nonmotorized play. Sax wanted everyone who visits a national park to become a naturalist.

Naturalist, of course, is a broad term. It can be used to describe leaders of the environmental movement, but just as likely characterizes people who want no more than to be left alone in a natural setting. When these reclusive naturalists do step up their activism, it usually is to preserve a wetland or prairie plot in their own bioregion and not to save the rainforests or the coral reefs. The exception, of course, is when the rainforest or the reef *is* their bioregion.

In my immediate circle, the term "naturalist" usually refers to the people who teach children about natural ecosystems. Occasionally they are the people who dance wildly in the moonlight and commune with the tree spirits. I have worked alongside naturalists who were both teachers of children and friends with the tree spirits, and then one of my responsibilities as their supervisor was to discourage them from being both at the same time. While I valued having quirky spiritually minded naturalists as colleagues, I needed them to tone down their eccentricities when they were with the kids. From my position as an administrator, I did not want my staff offending the mainstream principals, classroom teachers, and parents who went out of their way to support our programs.[6]

I consider myself a naturalist in several senses of the word, but I still sometimes allow the routines of urban life to overwhelm all of them. That is why time in the wilderness is so important. It sometimes takes a few days in the backcountry for my naturalistic tendencies to reemerge, but they always do. They present themselves as an awareness of my surroundings and a sense of calm. I usually don't notice the exact moment when the stress of the city sloughs off, but I think that's what happens. One morning about three days into a trip I will crawl out of my tent and just feel more alert. The various shades of green appear more vivid. The temperature gets measured by the tingle on my skin, not by a thermometer or a weather report. If the full orb of the sun is above the horizon when I crawl out of my sleeping bag, I feel I've already missed out on part of the day. "Burning daylight" sounds ridiculous when applied to city life, but makes complete sense in the backcountry.

When I was teaching at the university level, I saw the same quiet naturalist awareness and calm in recent graduates who would return to campus to tell me about their jobs as wilderness trip leaders or environmental center naturalists. These former students were unable to describe their work without breaking into big smiles, and I always saw a self-assuredness in them that was not there when they were still in school. Most of these young adults earned little more than room and board, yet thought they were living the dream.

The first six chapters of this book are built around nature writing. Nature-related literature is not a substitute for time in nature. It is a complement. (Interestingly, it also is usually a compliment.) At its very best, nature writing interprets the significance of experiences in nature when we fail to see it for ourselves. Because Thoreau, in *Walden*, wrote about resisting the animalistic urge to pounce upon a woodchuck and tear into its flesh, we better understand that we remain part of wild nature and, at the same time, distinct from her.[7] Because Willa Cather, in *O Pioneers!*, poetically described the land opening up to Alexandra Bergson when she looked upon it lovingly, we understand that nature speaks to us more willingly when we are ready to listen.[8]

When we read good nature writing, it usually is not so much a fresh idea as a confirmation of an insight we've developed on our own. In those instances, an accomplished wordsmith has described our thoughts better than we were able to do. After a certain age we shouldn't need others to validate our deepest feelings, but there is no downside to having the likes of Thoreau or Cather agree with us.

Part II

Sketches Here and There

Although it sometimes goes unnoticed, the two most common versions of *A Sand County Almanac* have slightly different subtitles. The subtitle of the Oxford University Press edition is "And Sketches Here and There."

7

Wisconsin East
A Small Square of Red

I WAS FIVE YEARS OLD, PLAYING ALONE IN OUR FRONT YARD. I REMEM-ber my exact age because it was the summer before I was to start kinder-garten. A huge woodpecker flew into the yard, sunk its zygodactyl[1] toes into the largest trunk of our three-pronged paper birch, and pecked into the tree a few times before departing as quickly as it had come. I knew the names of most of the common birds in our neighborhood, and one of my favorites was the redheaded woodpecker. The woodpecker I had just seen had lots of red on its head, but whereas the wingspan of a normal red-headed woodpecker is similar to that of a robin, this bird's span was twice that. I ran into the house to tell my mom I'd just seen the world's largest redheaded woodpecker. She was too busy ironing clothes to show any in-terest, and I went back outside hoping the bird would return. It never did.

Six years later, I went trout fishing with my dad in northern Wisconsin. The trout fishing of my childhood is not the trout fishing depicted in mov-ies. There were no wide vistas, no graceful casts with a fly rod, no evoc-ative glimpses of fish rising to the fly. Instead there were hordes of mos-quitoes and an impenetrable understory that snagged my fishing line and knocked the baseball cap off my head.

On days when my dad did not have a specific trout stream in mind, he drove the backroads until we came across an unexplored creek. These tiny streams were always heavily wooded and small. As far as my dad was concerned, if the alders growing on opposite banks did not meet in the middle, the water was big enough to fish. On this particular day, he had at least picked a creek that flowed beneath an actual bridge as it passed under the road. As often as not, we fished creeks so small they merited only culverts. Had Norman Maclean fished the waters I fished as a kid, he'd have written a very different book.

Trout fishing purists can rattle off a dozen ways trout fishing is different from and better than every other kind of fishing. For me as a kid, trout fishing had only one difference of note; it was always done *alone*. After grabbing our poles, my dad headed upstream, and I went down. It was always my dad going up and me going down. Each of us honed our skills accordingly. For me, it was easier to cast into a pool from the upstream side because the current would gently carry my live bait into a deep hole or quiet eddy. Fishing from the upstream side of a pool, however, made it easier to spook the fish. I could not walk in the water at all, because if I did, my sloshing would stir up the creek bottom and send sticks and silt into a potential fishing hole. The detritus would put wary trout on alert, and I had no choice but to find a new location farther downstream for which to put in a line.

On this particular outing, I bushwhacked through the alder brush for a quarter mile in hopes of finding a stretch of water where no one else had been. I can't tell you the name of the creek. I remember it ran into the Peshtigo River somewhere in Wisconsin's Forest County, but that only narrows down the possibilities to fifteen or more different tributaries. After fishing for only a few minutes, an otter bounced in from somewhere and started fishing directly across the creek from me. With miles of unoccupied water to choose from, it had to have intentionally chosen a spot close to me. It took only seconds for it to dive into a pool, grab a creek chub, and then sit in the shallows on the opposite bank to chew on its catch. At the time, I thought fishing with an otter was kinda cool, but not a big deal. When I met up with my dad at the end of the day, I told him I'd seen an otter, but didn't even mention that the otter and I had fished together.

In recalling these two encounters, the one with the woodpecker and the one with the otter, I realize I'd misinterpreted both. I now know that the bird I'd seen as a five-year-old was a pileated woodpecker, not a redheaded woodpecker—and while seeing a pileated is a treat, it is not all that unusual. The otter encounter, on the other hand, was a real once-in-a-lifetime experience. The incident I thought was unique was not, and the one I almost took for granted is unlikely to ever happen again. In looking back upon these two memories, I treasure each equally, but for different reasons.

The woodpecker sighting is a reminder to value the unusual, but not necessarily the rare, events in nature. When I was a kid, nature surprised me on a weekly basis—and often in my own yard. A giant woodpecker on a birch tree, a hundred fireflies in the backyard, a garter snake curled up under the leaky faucet on the side of the house. Now I am an old man, and it has been a while since I've been stunned by nature in my own yard. The last time I can think of is the night two summers ago when nighthawks dive-bombed the neighborhood.

The otter encounter is a reminder that special things occur when we spend enough time in the natural world. I am not sure whether it is a good thing or a bad thing, but the days of me having once-in-a-lifetime experiences in nature and not recognizing them as such are over. If something happens today that has never happened in my first six and a half decades of life, I take notice. Paradoxically, one of the reasons I was able to fish with an otter at all may have been because I did not appreciate what was going on. I was almost nonchalant about it. I am sure the otter saw me before I saw it, and I assume it was watching for my reaction. The reason it kept coming was because I never changed what I was doing the whole time it was there. I fished before it came, I fished as it approached, and I fished after it parked directly across the creek from me. If the same thing was to happen now, I would crouch down and freeze, and the change in my behavior might alert the animal that something was up. My casual childhood reaction to the otter's presence put me, as far as the otter was concerned, in the same stead as the red squirrels and woodcocks. I was not a threat like the other bipeds it had seen on the creek. An expert in otter behavior might find a flaw in my thinking, but I'm sticking to it because I believe kids have encounters with nature that adults cannot.

Mountains Speak for Themselves

In experiential education theory, there is a concept sometimes called "the mountains speak for themselves." It originally came from Stephen Bacon out of the Colorado Outward Bound School as a reaction to the over-debriefing he sometimes saw among his coleaders.[2] Every time something interesting happened on a wilderness trip, the tendency of some leaders was to gather everybody together to talk about it. The leaders' actions were well-intentioned. Nature had provided a valuable lesson, and the people in charge wanted to make sure every participant, down to the least reflective person in the group, appreciated the significance.

Still, there are some events so exceptional that gathering everybody together actually detracts from the moment. I can imagine Bacon and a group coming up over a mountain pass and getting their first look at the next range of mountains on the horizon. Bacon's coleader instinctively brought the group together to discuss the beauty of the great view, and Bacon wanted to scream, "Hey, what are you doing? The mountains speak for themselves!"

I am enamored with moments in nature that need no explanation. I like having them, and I like recalling them. I am sure I read too much into them, but not because I care about interpreting the emotions they stir within me. I just want to know how to have more of them and, if possible, how to create similar experiences for my family and my students. I have more to say about great moments in nature, especially about making them happen for others, but that will come in the next chapter. For now, I want to recount one more childhood memory.

A Small Square of Red

One afternoon my dad pulled off the road at a bridge. Even from the car, I could see that the current in the river flowed too slowly for trout, so I guessed he just wanted to walk out on the bridge to gaze at the water. When I was a kid, I got carsick a lot, so any reason to get out of the car for five minutes was welcome. Directly below us on the bridge a small sandbar had formed in the eddy behind an abutment. On the sandbar sat a half dozen leopard frogs. I was about to clamor down the riverbank to chase the frogs when my dad told me to stay up on the bridge. He gave me the car keys and asked me to grab my fishing pole. This was back in the days when you still needed a key to open the trunk. He said he thought there was a plastic bucket there, too—and if so, I should bring that also. When I returned with the pole and the bucket, he pulled a red handkerchief out of his pocket and used his jackknife to cut a small square of red material out of one corner. My family did not have much money at the time, and my dad was cheap. I remember being surprised he'd intentionally put a hole in his handkerchief. He put the red square on the bare hook of my pole and told me to gently lower it in front of the outermost frog. I did, and the frog immediately lunged at the red material. It hooked itself, and I reeled it in like a fish. I put the frog in the bucket, and my dad covered the top of the bucket with the handkerchief. The lunging frog surprised me, but no more so than the fact that none of the other frogs moved when their companion was lifted to the heavens. Had I crept down the bank, I might have caught one frog before the rest jumped into the river. With my fishing pole, I was able to lower the red lure six times and catch every one.

With six frogs in the bucket, my dad asked me what I wanted to do with them. I said I wanted to put them back. I walked down the embankment and gently poured leopard frogs into the river. I knew that the correct way to release fish was to humanely set them in the water, not toss them—and I assumed the same principle applied to frogs. Then we got back in the car and drove home.

I once thought all environmentalists were born of nature-related play in childhood. I now know this not to be true. There are dedicated environmentalists who have never spent much time outdoors. Their commitment to the natural world comes from a source other than personal experience in the wild. I revised my theory to thinking it was environmental educators, not necessarily all environmentalists, who played in nature when they were young. This too is incorrect. I have now met a handful of excellent environmental educators who can only be described as hardcore urbanites. These city-bred educators tend to focus more on sustainability than nature-based programming, but they are as dedicated to the protection of natural resources as the naturalists who chased butterflies as kids. I still believe many people find their environmentalism in youthful outdoor play, but the strongest definitive statement I dare to make now is that people who played in nature as children continue to play in nature as adults.

8

California With a Touch of Maine
Tide Pools East and West

THE PREVIOUS ESSAY ABOUT WOODPECKERS, OTTERS, AND FROGS DE-
scribed three childhood memories that left an impact on me. Not only
did they nudge me toward a career as a naturalist, but they inspired me
to make sure my work as a naturalist generated memorable experiences
for children.

The desire to make special moments in nature is common among environmental educators. Steve Van Matre went so far as to consider it the finishing touch to all good nature-based programming. He called it the
magic. Lessons about sustainability and ecology are important, but it is
the magic that leaves a lasting impression. In *Earth Education*,[1] Van Matre
recounts the story of being at Disney World around Christmastime and
watching the Christmas parade in the Magic Kingdom. When Santa Claus
was about to pass by, a man directly across from Van Matre on the parade
route pulls a makeshift sign out of his jacket. The sign reads "Richard."
The man holds the sign above, but a little bit behind, a young boy standing in front of him. The man then points down to the boy. Santa notices
the man, the boy, the sign—then immediately shouts, "Hello, Richard!"
Van Matre used this as an example of the creative tinkering naturalists can
use to turn good programming into events never forgotten.

As far as I know, there are two distinct ways for educators to increase the likelihood of a memorable experience. The first is the gentle manipulation exemplified by Van Matre's Disney World example. It is basically adding spice or an element of surprise to an event where it otherwise might not occur. The second way, much less certain of success, is to simply put people in situations where the remarkable has a chance to occur on its own. Nine times out of ten, maybe ninety-nine times out of a hundred, nothing special happens, but when it does, it is remarkable. The very best experiences in nature always come with an element of luck, but naturalists can take steps to increase the odds. An interesting thing about this second category of experience is that educators might create a magical moment for someone and not even be aware that it happened. These are the events where an educator gets an email from a former student ten years after the fact that reads something like, "I just wanted you to know the reason I went into environmental education as a career was because of the time you took us [fill in the blank]." It takes only one such letter or email every few years to justify an entire career in teaching.

Gentle Deception

My favorite example of clever and gentle manipulation leading people to a memorable experience in nature was done to me, not by me. I was camping in Maine's Acadia National Park. Acadia is a wonderful place and the easternmost point in the US. Had I awakened before dawn while I was there, I could have been the first person in America to see the sun that day.

One evening I was eating dinner at my Acadia campsite, and a young interpretive naturalist came by to tell me she was about to give a slideshow in the campground's amphitheater. This was in the late 1970s, which meant a slideshow actually included a slide carousel, a projector, and, very likely, a second person standing behind the projector to advance the slides. I attended the presentation, although I was more interested in observing the young woman's delivery than learning anything about the park. It was obvious she was a seasonal ranger, probably a college student. Just from the brief encounter with her when she walked into my campsite, I could tell she was thrilled to have a summer job at a national park.

As I expected, the inexperienced ranger's presentation had more passion than polish, but her enthusiasm was enough to hold the audience's attention. At one point in the slideshow, there was a photo of a vertical piece of rock on a craggy shoreline. An ocean wave had just crashed into the pillar, and water shot high into the air. Without a clear point of reference, it was hard to judge the exact height of the rock or the spray, but my guess was twenty, maybe even thirty feet. Members of the audience immediately wanted to know the location of the photo. The young interpreter told us that it was easy to find, and if we parked at Sand Beach on Park Loop Road, then walked south along the shoreline for about a mile and a half, we'd see the rock and very likely see waves crash into it.

The next morning I drove to Sand Beach to find the rock for myself and discovered three other families from the previous evening's presentation had the same idea. We walked together along the rocky coastline, explored a few tide pools, and watched a cormorant repeatedly dive and surface directly alongside us. It was low tide, and two kids picked up any starfish not firmly attached to a rock and threw it into the ocean to make sure a less conscientious tourist didn't steal it for a souvenir. With all of the interesting distractions on the shoreline, it took us over an hour to reach our destination. The tall rock and the crashing waves were all that we had hoped, and the scene was beautiful.

What the young interpretive naturalist had failed to tell us, however, was that the magnificent rock was barely fifty yards from the next parking lot down the road. From this second parking lot, a lazy tourist could have seen the watery display through the windshield of his car. As we turned around to walk back to our vehicles, one of the young starfish tossers told her parents exactly what I was thinking. I overheard her say, "I'm glad the lady from last night tricked us."

My own example of a similar educational deception, although I prefer to call it an omission, was during my years as a naturalist in the California redwoods south of San Francisco.[2] The name of the center was SMOE, or San Mateo Outdoor Education. The County of San Mateo is the entire

San Francisco Bay Peninsula other than the city of San Francisco itself. Most sixth graders in the county, at least those attending publicly funded schools, came to my camp and stayed with my staff and me for five days of nature study. One entire day of their visit was spent on the coast hiking salt marshes and exploring tide pools. Just before lunch on their beach day, the bus usually stopped at a place known as Pebble Beach (not the Pebble Beach of golf fame), and the kids and the naturalists hiked along a mile of shoreline from Pebble Beach to a second beach named Bean Hollow. At Bean Hollow, the naturalists cooked up hotdogs and grilled cheese sandwiches for lunch while the kids played on the beach and got a break from their day of oceanside lessons.

Kids loved the hike from Pebble Beach to Bean Hollow. The shoreline was a natural obstacle course, and the entire hike was climbing onto and then jumping off large rocks between short sections of water-hardened sand. Just offshore, sometimes no more than thirty feet from where we hiked, were small outcroppings of rock that poked up out of the ocean. Platforms on these outcroppings always contained dozens of harbor seals. The naturalists, because they recognized the rotund camouflaged bodies for what they were, saw the seals from a long way off, but never pointed them out. We would always be right on top of them before one of the kids would yell, "Hey, look! Seals! Those rocks aren't rocks. They're seals." Many of the kids, even though they had lived within thirty miles of the coast all of their lives, had never seen a seal in its natural habitat. Not only did these sixth graders see wild seals for the first time, but because the naturalists kept their mouths shut, they were the ones to discover them.

Increasing the Odds

The second way to create magic in the outdoors is to put people in situations where there is a chance something grand will occur. For me, one example of this second approach stands out above all others. It also answers the question of whether a memorable experience for a student might also be a once-in-a-lifetime experience for the teacher.

The highlight of SMOE's day at the ocean was always the tide pools. On the evening prior to the kids' trip to the coast, one of the naturalists conducted a slideshow about tide pooling. The presentation included rules for safely wandering out on the rocks, etiquette for handling the tide pool creatures and their homes, and photos of the kinds of animals the kids might find if they gently overturned rocks and looked carefully. Some of the animals were sure bets—anemones, barnacles, urchins, hermit crabs. Others required more careful searching—chitons, starfish, and rock crabs. Still others were rare finds, so unusual that our first-year naturalists had yet to see them even after several months on the job. Examples of these animals included brittle stars, sea slugs, and octopi. The slideshow got kids excited about the day, and it eliminated the need for any formal instruction once we arrived at the tide pools. In an earlier essay, I wrote that visiting places makes me want to read books about them. *Cannery Row* was my favorite novel during my two years of tide pooling at SMOE. I even enjoyed the movie, which apparently most Steinbeck fans did not.

One week it was my turn to present the slideshow. Immediately after it was over and the kids were filing out of the nature center to return to their cabins for bed, John, a boy who had been totally engaged with just about everything we'd done from the moment he stepped off the bus, said to me, "Tomorrow I'm gonna find an octopus."

I immediately regretted having the octopus in the photo array. "I'll help you look," I replied, "but I've gone to the tide pools once a week for two years, and I've only seen an octopus once. Don't be disappointed if we don't find one."

The next day we hit the tide pools at low tide. Most of the kids casually peeked under a few rocks and were satisfied to find dozens of hermit crabs and a few anemones and starfish. John worked a distance away from the other kids and carefully turned over rock after rock. There were four other staff members on the outing, so I was able to give John the extra one-on-one attention he deserved. I also was the bus driver for our beach days and, therefore, the de facto person in charge. Usually a group spent about an hour at the tide pools, but on that day I kept stretching out our stay. Even the other naturalists started looking at me questioningly as one hour stretched into an hour fifteen, then an hour and a half. Finally I yelled for everyone to start heading back to the bus. When everyone except John and I had climbed up to the parking lot and I was ready to tell John he had to give up, he pointed and quietly said, "There."

I looked to where he was pointing. The tiny arm of a small octopus reached out from under one rock to wrap itself around a second smaller rock. John didn't say, "I told you so," but he gave me a smile that more or less said it. I told him octopi were fast and able to escape through very small cracks, but if we built a small rock wall around the octopus before we lifted the rock it was hiding under, we had a chance it might stay in place long enough for us to get a quick look.

We built the circular wall. I told John it was his discovery, so it was his job to gently lift the rock. I also told him to get into a position where he could immediately see what was underneath, because I was pretty sure that the octopus would be gone in a flash. John lifted the small rock, but the octopus did not move. I was surprised, but John just grinned. After thirty seconds with no movement, I told him to sit quietly as I left to get the rest of the kids off the bus.

I walked up to the bus, told the kids that John had found his octopus, and if they returned to the tide pools quietly, they might get a look, too. The kids were great. They shifted into silent mode even before they stepped off the bus. Fifty kids circled the small rock cage John and I had constructed. Thirty-five years have passed since that incident, and I still marvel at how calmly John took in the whole experience. To the other kids, he was hero for the day. Even to the staff, he'd done something remarkable, but he remained focused on his exceptional find. After all of the kids had taken their turn at the front of the circle and had a good look at the octopus, I told John he could stay down in the tide pool until the other kids were up near the bus. Once there were only a few kids left to board, he gently took down the wall so the octopus could get out without slipping through a crack. Then he joined the rest of us.

John and the octopus were a fantastic moment for me as an educator. For John, I will never know whether it left an impression. From his calm demeanor, it might have had almost no effect at all. Conversely, it might have been the California equivalent of the time I fished with an otter, meaning it was one of a series of experiences that led to a career in environmental education. If John grew up to major in economics and work as a consultant on Wall Street, I don't want to know about it.

First Time Birding

I have one other quick story that relates to the topic at hand. I tell it because it points out how worthwhile it can be to simply bring novices to nature, because no one can predict which experience turns into something special.

When I first moved to Northern California, several months before I got the SMOE naturalist position, I took a job selling backpacking gear at a North Face store in San Francisco's Stonestown Mall. One of my co-workers was a woman named Mary. Mary's primary job was as a freelance editor, but she worked at North Face just enough hours to get the employee discount on clothing.

One day she asked me, "You're a birdwatcher, aren't you?" I was momentarily confused, but then remembered I'd once mentioned to her that my life list of bird sightings had increased by fifty species within a month of moving to the West Coast. I had spent enough time with good birdwatchers to know I should not call myself a birder, but I told her I went to look at birds fairly often. She then explained she'd just received a pair of binoculars as a gift and wondered whether I would take her birdwatching. When I asked her how much birding she'd done, she answered, "None."

I said, "In that case, we don't need to do anything elaborate. We can see plenty of birds just walking around Golden Gate Park."

The following Saturday we met outside the natural history museum in the park and started wandering. Even though Mary had lived her entire life in the Bay Area, it became obvious she didn't know a scrub jay from a western bluebird. She was excited to put names to birds she'd seen since she was a little girl. As for me, I was enjoying one of the few times in my life when I was birding with someone less knowledgeable than I was.

After the first half hour, I stopped telling her the names of birds and instead helped her find them in one of the two bird guides I'd brought along. We saw a new bird pecking in the grass adjacent a wooded area. Mary pointed at a page in my *Peterson Guide* and exclaimed, "Oh my God! Is that the bird?"

When I confirmed that it was, she said, "Last weekend I was babysitting the two-year-old son of a friend of mine. We were eating lunch at a park in Berkeley, and a bird was working up the courage to grab some of the food scraps the boy was dropping on the ground. The boy pointed at the bird and said, 'Tooey.' I corrected him and said, 'No, it's a birdy.' But he just kept saying, 'Tooey, tooey,' and I kept telling him, 'Birdy, birdy.' The bird that we saw that day was the same as the picture in this book. It was a towhee. I'm telling the little boy 'birdy,' and he's teaching me the name of the bird."

9

Minnesota
Night of the Quintze

THE MOST PRISTINE NATURE I'VE EVER EXPERIENCED FIRSTHAND IS the Boundary Waters Canoe Area in January. This may surprise backcountry users who paddle the crowded BWCA[1] in the summer, but visitors to the Boundary Waters are as seasonal as lightweight sleeping bags. From the opening day of walleye season until Labor Day, the Boundary Waters is the most popular designated wilderness[2] in the US. In the winter, however, the place is empty. On my four winter trips to the area, not only did I not see anyone outside my immediate group, but I knew I wouldn't see anyone.

I have been on summer and autumn wilderness trips where I did not encounter human beings outside my own traveling party. What sets winter camping apart, whether in the Boundary Waters or in other wilderness areas, is not merely the absence of people. It is the absence of the evidence of people. Most of the impact of summer users is buried underneath three feet of unbroken snow. Campfire scars, occasional pieces of litter, even the welcome stack of dry firewood left behind by the previous guest in a campsite are nowhere to be seen. In the Boundary Waters in the winter, I can think of only two signs of a human presence not hidden away until spring. One I like, and the other I don't.

The likable indicator of people having passed through is the snow-covered portage trails. In the summer, portages are crowded with people and often muddy. They are the backbreaking work between periods of peaceful paddling. In the winter, portages transform themselves into enticing invitations to another world. They become physical manifestations of the metaphorical road not taken. If there are no ski tracks on the portage trails, and there never are unless I've made them myself, these meandering paths symbolize solitude better than no trail at all. In the summer, portages are the worst part of the trip. In the winter, I think they are the best.

The second indicator of a human presence, while not ugly, bothers me. I hesitate to mention it, because once pointed out, it is hard to unsee. Readers can skip this paragraph if they don't want to know what it is. In the Boundary Waters, the other sign of summer visitors visible during the winter is the human browse line that radiates out for thirty to sixty feet from the more popular campsites. This is the result of campers tearing the dead lower branches off live trees. Rather than getting into their canoes to scavenge other shorelines for downed firewood, lazy campers snap off the wood most readily available. Harvesting standing wood is justifiable in life and death situations, but otherwise violates minimum impact standards. In the winter, I camped directly atop the ice on the lakes and did not use the designated campsites, so if not for the unnatural openness caused by the browse lines, I doubt I would have noticed the summer campsites at all.

And then there is the silence. Even the delightful sounds normally associated with the Northwoods are nowhere to be heard. Gentle waves lapping the shoreline are for other seasons of the year. So too is the rustling of birch and aspen leaves, and anyone who goes to the Boundary Waters to hear loons would best come back in May.

I can count on one hand the common sounds of the BWCA in winter. There is the wind through the conifers, the crackling of the campfire, the crunch of cross-country skis breaking trail through crusty snow, the chattering of chickadees first thing in the morning, and for the lucky few, the howl of the wolves. There may be no quiet so complete as the dead silence immediately following the howl of a lone wolf on a winter's night.

James Lee Burke once described a Louisiana bayou as swollen with silence.[3] As much as I like the imagery, it doesn't apply to the Boundary Waters in the winter. "Swollen with silence" has a heaviness to it, the auditory equivalent of a hot humid day that weighs a person down. BWCA silence is weightless in comparison, usually something a person does not even notice until he or she stops to listen for it. Frigid winter air is so crisp that noise carries for miles, but even then there is nothing to hear. The same winter forces that plummet temperatures and steal daylight create a world of silence.

The best (i.e., the least cold) way to winter camp in the Boundary Waters is to build and sleep in quintzes. Quintzes, sometimes called poor man's igloos, are hollowed out piles of snow that look like something the neighborhood kids would dig after the snowplow goes by. On my first organized winter camping trip, quintzes were our group's primary shelters. On our initial night in the backcountry, eleven of us slept in tents, but once we'd skied to our base camp on the morning of day two, we built three quintzes on the ice in a small bay north of Sawbill Lake. The hope was that the R-value of the quintzes would keep us warmer than the tents had the night before.

On the evening we were to try out our new accommodations, our group circled the campfire and talked about the day. Leo McAvoy, our lead instructor, repeatedly encouraged us to step away from the campfire to check out the stars, but none of us moved. The campfire produced light pollution, but it was also the only source of heat. It would have taken a show of the Northern Lights to pull most of us away from the fire, and there were no Northern Lights that night. I'd been on other outdoor trips with Leo during other times of the year, and he'd allowed only very small campfires for fear of disturbing the wilderness experience of others who might be in the immediate area. The fire that night was massive by McAvoy standards. We were in the middle of the Boundary Waters in late January, so we were not going to be bothering anyone.

One by one we called it a night and retreated to our sleeping bags. I was the first person in my quintze to leave the fire, so I set up in one of the two outer positions on our four-person sleeping platform of packed snow. Taking one of the roomier spots in the center of the quintze would have partially blocked the door for my three bunkmates when they came in, but in retrospect, I should have done it anyway. Quintzes are domes, so the outer sleeping positions have lower ceilings and are more cramped than the ones in the middle. By the time all four of us had crawled into our sleeping bags, my right shoulder was tight against the curved wall of our shelter and my left shoulder brushed the guy next to me.

Because the insides of quintzes are white and sparkly, one candle or one flashlight will softly light up the entire space. Without a light source, however, the interiors are as dark as caves. Sometime during the night I reached into the blackness and felt the bend of the ceiling only a foot and a half from my face. I panicked. Until that moment, I hadn't known I was afraid of confined spaces. Wearing only polypropylene long underwear, a balaclava, and a pair of wool socks, I clamored over the guy next to me and bolted for the door. After only a few seconds outside, I'd regained my wits, but now was at risk of freezing my fingers and toes. We'd brought thermometers to compare the temperature inside and outside of our shelter, but I didn't need a thermometer to know it was well below zero on the Fahrenheit scale. I didn't want to return to the quintze, but I crawled back in to retrieve the rest of my clothes and all of my sleeping gear. The other three campers were now wide awake with their flashlights on, wondering what had just happened. The two guys in the center were sitting up. The third guy, who was in a position similar to mine but on the opposite side of the quintze, did not have the headroom to sit up. He was packed in as tightly as I had been.

I told my sleeping partners I was fine, but I was going to pitch a tent and sleep outside. I asked them to go back to bed, but all three got dressed and helped me set up the tent. As far as they could tell, I'd lost my mind and could not be left alone. One of the three even offered to leave the relative warmth of the quintze to sleep with me in the tent. I convinced him that the last thing I wanted just then was another person within five feet of me. Three rugged outdoorsmen literally tucked their crazed bunkmate into bed and stood outside my tent in the cold until they were sure I'd stopped shivering. Only then did they return to their own sleeping bags to get some sleep.

I do not winter camp anymore, although the main reason has only a little to do with claustrophobia. I just got tired of always being not quite warm enough. Hardier souls than I claim winter camping is hardly more difficult than late autumn camping, but I disagree. Every minute that does not include vigorous exercise is a minute trying to keep warm. Cold weather makes my knees ache, and lately I've been listening a lot more to my knees.

I like the idea of winter camping more than I like the actual camping. In theory, winter camping provides everything summer excursions do and offers it with greater intensity. More challenge, more natural beauty, and most of all, more solitude and quiet. All of that would be wonderful if it wasn't so cold.

Yet in spite of the constant cold, giving up winter camping was not an easy decision. Like most backcountry users, I am borderline addicted to the knowledge that if I go into the wild on my own, I have to get out on my own. I was never in any danger on that night in the Boundary Waters, but had things gone badly, I fantasize my companions would have left my body on the ice, either to feed the wolves or to sink to the bottom of the lake come spring. All wilderness areas in all seasons are capable of generating thoughts of dying on our own terms, but the starkness of the wild in the *dead* of winter makes the case more emphatically than the relative comfort of summer. It is not coincidence that the most famous line about confronting death in the wilderness comes from the poet laureate of the wintry North, Robert Service. He wrote:

> The nameless men who nameless rivers travel,
> And in strange valleys greet strange deaths alone.[4]

What is it that accompanies such thinking? Self-reliance comes to mind, but it could just as well be machismo, temporary insanity, or the longing for freedom. I think I will go with the last of those emotions. With complete solitude comes a sense of freedom.

While I was writing this essay about winter camping in the BWCA, I wanted another word for wilderness. Not able to come up with one on my own, I went to the Oxford English thesaurus, but every synonym for wilderness was about desolation: uninhabited region, inhospitable region, uncultivated region, badlands, wasteland, neglected area, abandoned area, no-man's-land. I was seeking a word with positive connotations, so obviously none of these served my purpose. They left me wondering whether anyone had bothered to update that particular thesaurus entry since the Victorian era.

Out of curiosity, I also looked up the word "solitude" to see whether its synonyms were less bleak. They were not. Loneliness, solitariness, remoteness, isolation, seclusion, withdrawal, privateness, desolation, lonesomeness, and sequestration. Until the COVID pandemic, I didn't even know "sequestration" was a word.

I then wondered whether these unflattering interpretations of wilderness and solitude reflected a British perspective that did not carry over to the US. I put the Oxford thesaurus aside and looked up the same two words in the American-based Merriam-Webster thesaurus. The synonyms for wilderness were decidedly more positive: nature, open, open air, out-of-doors, and wild. Still not the seductive terms I was looking for to add to this essay, but at least they did not conjure up scenes from a Mad Max movie.

Solitude, however, did not fare as well. The Merriam-Webster description was even more depressing than the Oxford version. In addition to synonyms, the entry for solitude listed antonyms and what the thesaurus called "Related Words." The synonyms included aloneness, isolation, seclusion, and segregation. The antonyms were camaraderie, companionship, company, comradeship, and fellowship. The related words were confinement, incarceration, internment, and quarantine. If these were the only words to accurately describe "wilderness" and "solitude," I doubt even Jesus or Buddha would have sought them out.

Fortunately, or maybe fortuitously, I started reading Patricia Hampl's *The Art of the Wasted Day* on the same day I made my thesaurus search. Very early into the book, she quoted Schopenhauer, who wrote:

> A man can be himself only so long as he is alone; and if he does not love solitude, he will not love freedom; for it is only when he is alone that he is really free.[5]

Two hundred pages later, Hampl dedicated an entire chapter to solitude and began it by stating, "Solitude suggests not loneliness, but serenity, that kissing cousin of sanity."[6]

The difference between Hampl's and the thesauruses' interpretations of solitude reminded me of an incident while I was teaching at National Taiwan University back in the 1990s. My comprehension of Mandarin was barely better than survival level, so I had to teach in English. I was embarrassed that I forced Taiwanese students to speak a foreign language in their own country, so I rarely corrected their English.[7] Still, one day, after hearing the same error from just about every student in one of my classes, I told them, "In English, we don't say 'the nature.' We just say 'nature.'"

Of course, the students wanted to know the reason for this quirk in the language, and I had no idea. It was one of the students who figured it out. "Maybe," he said, "it is because nature is a concept, not an object. In English, 'the' is used with objects, but not with concepts. To say 'the tree' is good English; to say, 'the freedom' is not."

Other students immediately nodded their heads and agreed this was the rule that fit the situation. I stood dumbfounded in the front of the classroom because I didn't even realize there was such a rule.

Anyone whose first language is English and has spent time with people whose second language is English quickly discovers that graduates of English as a second language programs understand the whys of English better than native speakers. This makes logical sense but can be disconcerting, nonetheless. Assuming most of the people reading this book are native English speakers, how many of you knew about the "the" rule?

Language comprehension, of course, is more than a set of rules. There are countless exceptions to the rules, each exception with its own rabbit hole to fall into. As soon as I had wrapped my head around the "the" rule, I realized that my original statement about the use of "the" with "nature" was incomplete. There are, in fact, two kinds of nature. One is concrete, and one is ethereal; one is preceded by "the," and the other is not. I did not want to spend the next hour of class discussing the nuances of the English language with my Taiwanese students, so I moved on to another subject.

Still, it is not a pointless exercise to reflect upon the two kinds of nature—or the two kinds of wilderness or the two kinds of solitude. It is a good reminder of the role of each. In my former world of academics, I tended to focus on the loftier idealistic notions of these words, but never forgot that the ideals had no relevance without a sampling of the physical manifestations upon which the ethereal words were based. Wilderness has no meaning without *the* wilderness, nature no meaning without *the* natural world. I suppose it possible to reflect upon solitude without first experiencing *the* solitude of a natural area, but that is not an intellectual exercise I care to be part of. Even in years when my department's travel budget had been cut nearly to zero, my students and I frequently walked to the nearby marsh or the nearby urban forest to spend a little time in actual nature and, as much as possible, to experience a semblance of solitude.

A friend of mine once taught a college course titled Wilderness. In the first half dozen class meetings, he defined the term and began to discuss the role of wild places in the American consciousness. Three weeks into the semester, a student came up to my friend after class and asked, "Are we going to learn how to build a campfire in this course?" The student was asking the right question.

10

Iowa
The Birds of Iowa

WHEN I LIVED IN IOWA IN THE LATE 1980S, I SIGNED UP FOR A BIRD class. It met every Saturday for five weeks. I cannot recall a single thing about four of those meetings, but the other one will stick with me forever.

It was the day we focused on owls. In the morning, the class dissected owl pellets. Owls swallow their prey either whole or in big chunks. Their digestive tracts break down skin and muscle, but the birds must regurgitate undigested hair and bones. By dissecting the regurgitated pellets, a person can extract small bones and identify what the owl ate. In this context, I use the word "identify" loosely, because most of us can't differentiate the bones of a mouse from those of a vole or a mole or even a baby rabbit. The extent of the bone identification usually stops at "small rodent," and even that sometimes is wrong. A particular owl might have munched on a lizard or a bird along the way, but so long as the bones are wrapped in hair, we assume all of the remains are mammalian.

I dissected owl pellets with students in one of my own classes, so was a bit bored by this part of the workshop. After the dissection, however, the young naturalist in charge said, "Okay, now we'll go outside to look for pellets." As dumb as it sounds, it had never occurred to me that someone could actually search for owl pellets. The ones I used in my own classes came from a mail order biological supply house, and I never wondered where those pellets had come from.

The members of the class stepped out of the nature center building onto the grounds. After the naturalist had divided us into teams of two, he said, "If you want to find big pellets, go to the woods. That's where the great horned owls and barred owls roost. If you want to find little pellets, go into the field. Saw-whet and screech owls roost in the bushes there. In either place, look for bird excrement. The whitish droppings are easier to see than the gray-brown pellets, but where an owl poops is where it pukes."

All of the teams except my partner and I immediately headed for the woods. They wanted to find big pellets. My partner suggested to me that we'd have a better chance of finding pellets if we went where the other people weren't. The nature center's grassland was basically an old pasture, abandoned long enough to have interspersed patches of shrubbery among the expanse of herbaceous plants. As instructed, my partner and I walked from bush to bush looking for bird droppings. The grasses in the field were over a foot high, so if we saw any whitish excrement on the tips of the grass, we got down on our hands and knees, pushed the grass aside, and looked for pellets on the ground. After a dozen bushes, we were zero for twelve.

At one of the bushes there were fresh droppings on the tips of the grass, and my waning enthusiasm was momentarily restored. I immediately dropped to my knees and scoured the ground for pellets. It was then that my partner tapped me on the shoulder and pointed at the spot where the shrub was brushing the top of my head. I looked up and there, less than a foot away from my nose, was the owl. Like the Canada jays I often see in the Boundary Waters, the little saw-whet showed no fear and probably was curious about what this odd human was up to. After watching the little guy for longer than I would have thought possible, I carefully backed away, and my partner and I tracked down the other pellet hunters to show them our discovery.

Had it not been for my partner, I might have never seen the owl. If a four-year-old girl sees fresh bird poop, her first instinct is to look for the bird. Not me. I was so focused on finding owl pellets, I wasn't going to notice anything else. I should have been surprised at my lousy observation skills, but I wasn't. Blinder mentality has often been a problem for me. When I look for trout, I see only fish. When I look for eagles, I see only raptors. How many woodland flowers have I unintentionally stepped on because I was looking for spring warblers?

In natural areas, single-minded observation skills versus an open mind is a dilemma. I have walked with exceptional observers who seem able to do both at the same time, but I am not one of those people. A good antidote for excessive focus is to go to nature with children, the younger the better. Not only are kids more open because of their shortened attention spans, but their eyeballs operate much closer to the ground. They notice stuff that is knee high on an adult, and their observations result in a barrage of questions. "What's that bug?" "What's that flower?" "Why does that poop got hair in it?"

One time during my years as a naturalist in California I was in an ocean cove with kids looking for unusual pebbles. Suddenly everyone except me jumped up and made a beeline for a point of land that jutted out into the ocean. They all had seen California gray whales swimming north and wanted to get as close a look as possible. I, on the other hand, hadn't even noticed anything other than the small stones I was sifting through my fingers. In fairness to me, the whales were a long way off and little more than exposed backs and spouts in the distance. Still, I use the incident to remind myself that I shouldn't be so intent on pebbles at my feet I miss whales on the horizon.

11

Taiwan

Ascent of Jade Mountain

WHEN I TAUGHT AT NATIONAL TAIWAN UNIVERSITY, STUDENTS OCCA-
sionally invited me to join them on weekend backpacking trips. It was
kind of them to take me to places I would have a hard time getting to on
my own, but my presence served them as well. In 1991, *recreational* hiking permits in Taiwan were hard to come by, but the inclusion of a college professor on a backcountry application meant the students could
apply for an *educational* permit instead. Educational permits were pretty
much rubber stamped, whereas recreational permits had to be submit-
ted months in advance and usually went to the big mountain clubs and
licensed guides. Anyone could join these clubs and be included on the
permits, but it meant traveling the backcountry with a group of twenty
or more. If the students wanted to hike on their own in a much smaller
group, it was best to apply for an educational permit—and to get an educational permit, they needed a faculty member to go along.

Yushan (玉山), or Jade Mountain, is the highest point in Taiwan. Its
ascent is an interesting three-day challenge. Day one, at least for people
without a car or chartered bus, is taking a series of trains and buses to
reach Yushan National Park and the base of the mountain. Day two is a
hike to base camp at a place called Paiyun. Day three is getting up several

hours before dawn, eating a quick breakfast, and hiking to the summit to greet the sun. After the sunrise, there is the return to base camp to retrieve personal gear, followed by a quick descent of the mountain in an attempt to catch the last bus out of the park.

Day One

The trailhead for the ascent of Yushan is near the National Park interpretive center at Tatachia. It is here the bus dropped us off. A short walk from the bus stop is Tungpu Hostel, a small bunkhouse where hikers who arrive too late to start their trip up the mountain can spend the night. After a train ride from Taipei to Ershui, a spur line from Ershui to Shuili, a short walk from the Shuili train station to the town's bus station, and finally a bus ride to Tatachia, it was far too late in the day to start our ascent.

It was at the Tungpu Hostel I had my first taste of Chinese backpacking food. Our evening meal was backcountry hot pot, a rehydrated version of the popular northern Chinese huo guo (火鍋). Because Chinese cuisine dehydrates just about everything, light dry food for backcountry dining is easy to find. My hiking companions threw chicken bouillon cubes, garlic, tofu, plus dried mushrooms, dried squid, and dried seaweed into a pot of cold water. The backpacking stove was turned to high, and when the covered pot boiled over, they added a few fresh greens, let it simmer for another minute, and turned off the heat. We then gathered around the pot and ate communally with chopsticks. Each piece of food was dipped into a mixture of soy sauce and barbecue sauce before eating. In Chinese dining, soup usually comes after the main course, so the chicken stock left in the pot was poured into cups after the solid food had been eaten.

Just before bed we also had ginger soup. Ginger, to the Chinese, is considered a winter food, meaning it has a warming effect. Chunks of ginger were boiled in sugar water, and the broth drunk to fend off the cold mountain air. For reasons no one could explain to me, an old, shriveled chunk of ginger was supposed to work better than a fresh piece. A traditional Chinese doctor once told me ginger works pretty much like alcohol, meaning it has questionable value in terms of really keeping the body warm. It dilates the capillaries, rushing warm blood to the extremities. This gives the illusion of warmth, but allows heat to escape the body through the skin. Just as I sometimes do with alcohol, I ignored the fact that ginger was sapping me of body heat and simply enjoyed the sweet liquid as a pleasant nightcap.

Day Two

After breakfast the next morning, our small group began the all-day trek from Tatachia to base camp at Paiyun Hostel. Once away from the parking lot and the interpretive center, the trail almost, but not quite, matched the North American notion of wilderness. Other than the presence of high-country bamboo, the terrain was reminiscent of Montana's Beartooths, maybe even sections of California's Sierra Nevadas.

Still, two aspects of Chinese backpacking constantly reminded me I was not in the US. The most obvious difference between Taiwan and North America was the amount of litter in the backcountry. On a Taiwanese trail, it was every few feet, so prevalent that I never considered picking any of it up. My students knew, without me saying it, that litter bothered Western hikers, and they expressed embarrassment at the mess.

A second and more pleasant difference between wilderness travel in Taiwan and the US was the social aspect of the Taiwanese experience. In the US, American hikers go to lengths to avoid each other. They ask park rangers about the most popular routes and then go somewhere else. They politely say hello to other people on the trail, but rarely strike up lengthy conversations.

Taiwanese hikers are the direct opposite. They view backpacking as an opportunity to talk to like-minded strangers. Chinese landscape paintings usually have a lone walker hidden somewhere in the scenes of mountains and rivers, but in my experience, this does not represent real Taiwanese backcountry use. Part of the reason for the large number of people, of course, is the permit system where mountain clubs obtain permits for twenty, thirty, forty backcountry users. Even though these large groups split up into smaller groups of four or five while on the move, they rarely miss an opportunity to stop to talk to passing travelers. Te-jen, one of my hiking partners and the main organizer of our Yushan trip, described Taiwanese backpackers as ants on an ant trail, stopping to rub antennae before moving on. Most of the people we encountered were curious about the waiguoren, or the foreigner (外國人). On that particular weekend, I saw no other non-Asians on the mountain. Because of my limited Mandarin, I did not understand much of the conversations. Still, I understood the most common comments. "Does he speak Chinese?" "Why did he let the sun burn his nose?" "He looks like he can carry a lot."

Although the excessive friendliness disrupted my sense of solitude, it also put a unique spin on backcountry travel. For example, our trip up Yushan was in the late fall, and it was the last open weekend before the National Park Department was to close the trail for the winter. Several mountain clubs wanted to get in a final ascent, so Paiyun Hostel at the base camp was totally booked when the students arranged for our permit. This meant our group could still go to Paiyun, but would have to spend the night in tents instead of in the stone bunkhouse. Camping anywhere on the mountain other than Paiyun was not allowed.

Our team of six hiked in two separate groups. Because I was thirty-eight years old and the oldest by fifteen years, it was assumed I would be in the slower second group. When my threesome reached Paiyun, I was pleased to see that our other members had taken the initiative to pitch the tents ahead of our arrival. Their good intentions, however, had brought out a man from inside the hostel. Wei-sheng, the only male in our small group other than me, had pitched one of the two four-person Timberlines directly in front of the hostel door. The man was yelling at Wei-sheng, so I quickly ran up to tell him that we would move the tent.

But as usual when people are speaking Mandarin, I'd misinterpreted the situation. The man definitely wanted us to take down the tent, but not because it was in the way. Instead the man was demanding we come inside. Even though every bunk in the hostel was occupied, his sense of backcountry etiquette would not allow him to leave us outside when there was warmth and the company of eighty fellow hikers just inside. It meant that I ended up sleeping on a five-foot-long table with one of my students on the floor beneath me, but Te-jen explained that it would have been rude for us to decline the man's invitation.

Day Three

After a few sleepless hours on the short table, I rose with my companions, ate hot cereal, donned headlamps, and, at 3:15 in the morning, started up the trail. We were not the first team out of Paiyun, but we were well ahead of the crowd. I soon discovered that the hostel sat just below the tree line, and as we moved above the protection of the last conifers, the extra chill was enough to frost my beard and mustache. The grade also steepened, and what might have been an easy ascent in daylight was a bit treacherous in the dark. Overhead I saw the silhouette of a false summit against the stars, but still no hint of dawn. Looking back down the trail I saw the bobbing headlamps of other hikers from Paiyun zigzagging the switchbacks that cut through the last of the wind-beaten trees.

After two hours of hiking, we encountered something my students had told me to expect. A few hundred meters below the summit, handrails had been built into the side of the mountain. The grade along the only route to the top changed from a walk to a scramble, and a length of chain had been secured to the granite as a guide. Along one especially windy stretch, there was even a chain-link fence to keep hikers from falling off the mountain. As I grabbed the chain, I could feel the cold of the metal through my mittens. I wondered whether this manmade infringement of the otherwise untouched wilderness was necessary. There was no technical climbing on our predawn hike. It was merely two and a half hours of uphill trudging through the snow in the dark. How many of the people on the mountain were backpacking novices in need of something to grab onto?

I concluded that the answer to my question was a lot of them. With the convenience of mountain clubs, I realized that up to a third of the hikers probably were beginners and would have a hard time making the summit without the help of the railing. In spite of the elevation (nearly four thousand meters) and the two-day hike to the top, the trip was generally friendly to first timers. With clean mountain huts, leadership from the mountain clubs, the security of the handrails, and the social nature of the whole thing, I imagined that several mountain visitors who normally opted for the comfort of plush mountain resorts were tempted to move outside their comfort zones to scale the one peak that symbolized all that was wild in Taiwan.

So here these people were, maybe for the first time in their lives, experiencing the wilderness firsthand. No televisions, no phones, no automobiles, and no breakfast buffet in the hotel lobby. Beginners were bumping shoulders with the pristine because it was not so treacherous that it attracted only experienced hikers. If a handrail and a chain-link fence helped to get newcomers excited about the wilderness, these man-made intrusions were a compromise worth having.

Just shy of the top, we reached a fork in the snow-covered trail. To the south was the route to the true summit of the mountain. The path through the windblown snow in that direction already showed the tracks of the handful of predawn hikers who'd preceded us that morning on the climb. To the north was a separate route to a nearby secondary summit. It was only a few meters lower than its taller sister. Not a single set of footprints disturbed the snow in that direction. If we went south, we'd watch the sunrise from the highest point in Taiwan, but we'd do it with eighty other hikers. If we went north, we'd fall short of the top, but we'd have the sunrise to ourselves. We needed to pick a direction, and the students made it clear the choice was mine.

I knew immediately that, at least for this weekend, I wanted to give into the Taiwanese way of doing things. To have gone north in search of solitude would have meant I was asserting my American approach to a Taiwanese hiking experience. I sensed the students wanted to go south with everyone else, and I realized I did, too. The feeling of awe was going to suffer a bit, but I've experienced awe on other trips. Sharing wilderness with strangers was going to be a new experience. Although my limited Mandarin kept me from having lengthy conversations with anyone at the summit, there was a chance of a connection because we were sharing the prize at the end of a trek.

I expected the crowd on top of Yushan to take away from the intimacy of the sunrise, but it turned out not to be the case. There was a sense of oneness in shivering together and waiting for the first appearance of the sun over the range of mountains to the east. Although we'd hiked through fairly deep snow for most of the morning, strong wind had blown the summit bare. The peak was not a pointy little knob where all of us had to cram together. Rather it was a pile of granite blocks spread out over thirty meters. As people in groups of three or four reached the very top, they initially reunited with other members from their particular hiking clubs—but as soon as it became apparent the sun was about to show itself, everyone spread out and found individual spots from which to sit quietly as the sun came up. From the moment the upper edge of the sun first appeared on the horizon until the full orb was visible, I don't think a single word was said. Cameras clicked, but otherwise it was quiet.

Once the sun was completely up, the first group of hikers started their climb back down the mountain. My group dawdled a bit to avoid being part of the mass exodus. A man who I thought was about sixty years old walked up to me and asked in Mandarin, "Waiguoren, do you speak Chinese?" When I told him I spoke a little bit, he said in slow, simple words, "I am eighty-six years old. This is the first time I've ever seen the Yushan sunrise. You and I did this together." I realized I had made a mistake in presuming a crowd would diminish my experience atop Yushan. For the old man, the presence of other people had not diminished his sense of awe—and because of that man, it hadn't for me either.

Note: This chapter previously appeared in a slightly different form in "Chinese Backpacking: An Ascent of Jade Mountain," *Travel in Taiwan* 7, no. 12 (1993): 4–8, www.taiwaneverything.cc.

12

A Return to Taiwan
Old and American

IN THE SUMMER OF 2009, I ATTENDED AN ALL-DAY ENVIRONMENTAL education workshop in Taipei. The two presenters were from northern Europe. One was from Germany and the other Sweden. The audience was faculty and students from National Taiwan Normal University's Graduate Institute of Environmental Education. I was teaching at NTNU for the year, and I was the only American in attendance and the only person over fifty years old. The relevance of my nationality and my age will soon become apparent.

Although it might not have been explicitly stated by the facilitators, the overriding theme of the workshop was that the greening of a nation goes hand in hand with the country's environmental education. Mass transit, urban green spaces, solar energy, and recycling are not necessarily a direct result of environmental education, but the nations actively reducing their carbon footprint are also the countries most ardently promoting environmental ed. Conversely, governments not doing the first won't have much of the second. I finished the day believing Europe, at least Scandinavia and Germany, was ten years ahead of Taiwan and fifteen years ahead of the US in terms of sustainability and sustainability education.

The workshop was organized by and for the graduate students of the institute, so I kept in the background most of the day. During the closing question and answer session, however, I finally spoke up and said, "This has been excellent, but it has been entirely about sustainability. Where does outdoor recreation and a connection to nature fit into German and Swedish environmental education programming? During the entire eight-hour workshop, there was no mention of nature study or making sure that kids spend time outdoors."

The two men smiled at each other, and the Swedish guy indicated the German should field my question. The German facilitator turned to me and said, "We often get that question, and when we do, it always comes from someone who is old and American. We are happy there are people like you taking children into wild places, but both my colleague and I consider sustainability the present and the future of environmental education."

The German had worded his response well. If he had simply said that the environmental education pendulum in Europe had swung from nature-based education toward sustainability education, I would have thought nothing of it. But within his answer he had intimated that the rise of sustainability education was so apparent and so complete that only an over-the-hill, American naturalist still immersed in the old ways of doing things would even bother to question it. Not only was I out of touch, but I was out of touch because I was old and because I was from the US.

It took me a while to realize that my frustration with the man's answer was more than an overreaction to a personal rebuke. The criticism was an affront to my brand of environmental education, and for the first time, I felt a schism within my profession. I have never been part of the tedious discussions that try to differentiate outdoor education from environmental education from adventure programming from outdoor recreation. To me, that particular argument is little more than semantics. Each of these subdivisions has its unique features, but all have time in nature as a common denominator. As far as I am concerned, that is what matters.

Sustainability education is different in this regard. It is environmental education not necessarily built around a connection with nature. The United Nations' name for sustainability education is education for sustainable development (ESD). Thirty years ago, any educational approach with the word "development" in its name would have been dismissed by the sizable tree hugger wing of the environmental education profession. Now it is at the field's forefront.

Of course, I am not the first to remark on the distinction between education for sustainable development and old-school nature-based education. In environmental philosophy, for example, it is sometimes framed as ESD's anthropocentric bent in a profession that has been traditionally biocentric. Social anthropologist Helen Kopnina went so far as to say it was environmentalism's "elephant in the room."[1]

Still, to convince myself I was not fabricating a divide within environmental education where none existed, I asked myself the following questions. I am not overwhelmed with my answers, but it was a good exercise.

1. What about education for sustainable development makes me uncomfortable?

Of the five questions, this one is the easiest to answer. I could be wrong, but I consider environmental education a zero-sum game. I wish that was not the case, but environmental education receives only finite time in schools and in community programs. Sustainability education and nature-based education complement each other in terms of goals and content, but they are in competition with each other when it comes to face time with students. I worry that young people's relationships with the natural world will suffer if environmental education focuses primarily on sustainability.

2. Has the time for nature-based education passed?

To me, a personal connection with nature is as timeless as a tattered copy of *Walden*. If this belief prevents me from embracing ESD as much as I might, then I *am* an old codger who will be left behind by his own profession. And maybe that is okay. Twenty-first-century educators can do their thing, and I will do mine and the two approaches toward similar ends will each make an impact on young people's lives. In the opening line of *A Sand County Almanac*, Aldo Leopold wrote about people who can live without wild things and those who cannot. Maybe the same description applies to environmental educators. There are those who must teach in wild places and those who don't. I am fully aware I answered this question by referencing two books that are, like me, both old and American.

3. What if nature-based education did assume a secondary role to ESD?

If education for sustainable development takes precedence over nature-based education, fewer young people will grow up needing wild nature in their everyday lives. Fewer people will hike, birdwatch, canoe, and fish. For those who do not spend extended time in natural settings, love of nature will become an abstraction. Students of sustainability education will still work to save wetlands and forests and shorelines, but it may be because they believe in a theoretical concept of healthy ecosystems, not because they possess a personal connection to a specific piece of land or water. Many things are lost when a person does not have an individual relationship to the natural world, but the first thing that comes to mind is a oneness with a particular wild place.

4. Is the problem that I'm old?

Environmental education, at least in the US, is a young person's profession.[2] At the grassroots level where teachers most often interact directly with children, pay is lousy, hours are long, and young naturalists do the good work for a few years before moving on to jobs with less burnout. I am one of the lucky ones who got to continue in environmental education for his entire career by teaching it at the college level. My sense is that the new generation of American environmental educators is just as immersed in nature-based education as their elderly counterparts. I live in the Midwest, a region that still possesses a good quantity of wild places and rural landscapes. Young naturalists here may be more sensitive to matters of sustainability than I am, but have built sustainability alongside a foundation of nature-based programming.

5. Is it okay for environmental education in the US to be different from that in the rest of the world?

I have not personally experienced much environmental education outside of Taiwan and the United States, but it is obvious that education for sustainable development is more extensive in many countries than it is in the US. Conversely, I sense nature-based environmental education and outdoor recreation may be more common in the US than in places focusing on sustainability. If this distinction is correct, is it okay? In spite of America's return to the Paris Accords, it remains behind the curve on matters of climate change. Could part of the problem be the kind of environmental education we focus on? Americans may understand the basics of sustainability, but are slow to implement significant change. Conversely, we, in spite of inadequate funding, remain the model for the world in terms of national parks and wilderness protection. Do different countries have different kinds of environmental education, which then lead to different environmental priorities? My thinking keeps circling back to the same question, and it is this: Just because my environmentalism is tied to experiences in the outdoors, does this mean everyone's environmentalism should be?

This last point is an important one. So long as northern Europe and the United States and Taiwan and the rest of the world have some kind of environmental education, does it matter if they take different approaches? Maybe another way of asking the same question is to ask whether environmental education ought to be bioregional. A basic premise of bioregionalism is that there is no cookie-cutter approach to most environmental topics. Should environmental education in places with large tracts of undeveloped nature be different from environmental education in places where the population density is significantly higher? One thing I do know for sure is that lands supposedly protected forever can lose their protected status, so it is vital to have an educated citizenry who continually advocates for nature preservation. Again I feel like I'm talking about a zero-sum situation when there shouldn't be one. Both nature preservation and sustainability are vital, and I am asking myself where one should be given priority over the other.

In looking at my answers to these five questions, three thoughts came to mind. First of all, I *am* old in terms of attitudes about my profession. I initially went into environmental education so that I could live and work outdoors. As a young man, I could have been just as happy going into park management or logging or community-supported agriculture. I chose, maybe somewhat fell into, environmental education and immediately dove headfirst into the sustainability issues of the time (e.g., clean water, clean air, mass transit, overpopulation). They were just part of the job. Gradually, however, I moved away from sustainability education and focused almost exclusively on nature study. I literally and figuratively drew deeper into the woods and took my students with me. Environmentalist and poet Gary Snyder once observed that Buddhists sometimes find peace by hiding behind monastery walls and divorcing themselves from the problems of the world.[3] I know very little about Buddhism, but I recognize wild nature as my monastic hideaway. Maybe I taught about nature because I needed to be in nature myself—not necessarily because I believed it was the most important topic to be taught. I remember patting myself on the back for doing honorable work, but my motivations may have been as self-serving as the motivations of those who work primarily for big paychecks.

Secondly, a small part of me wonders whether time in nature hasn't become a luxury in the same way that art, music, and literature are luxuries. These joys happen to be the very things that define a culture, but they also can seem self-indulgent when the planet is at peril. I appreciate that there are people who firmly believe the importance of such amenities actually increases in times of crisis, but I am not one of them. At least in regard to climate change, is it time for old nature educators to put aside their passion for nature study and contribute more wholeheartedly to education for sustainable development?

Thirdly, I know that, in spite of a genuine fear I have about the kind of planet my daughter will have to live in, I remain *old* and *American* in terms of environmental education. For every argument as to why I should embrace ESD, I can come up with a justification for why nature-based education remains equally crucial. Fortunately, young contemporary American environmental educators are better aligned with ESD than I am. They effectively blend sustainability with nature appreciation and don't see why anyone would do it differently. They, along with the two German and Swedish educators in Taiwan, probably have it right. In environmental education, as in most other fields, it is time for baby boomers to step aside and let more progressive practitioners take over. As already stated, environmental education has always been a young man's and young woman's domain.

13

Ontario
Goodbye, Deadbroke Island

I WALKED ACROSS THE CAMPUS OF THE UNIVERSITY OF FLORIDA AND saw an alligator on the lawn near a small lake. I was taken aback, but the hundreds of students who were moving between classes hardly noticed. To these Floridians, the alligator garnered the same attention a squirrel would have back on my own campus. When I asked my host about everyone's indifference, he said, "Yeah, there are signs telling students not to sunbathe near the lake, but they do anyway."

When my daughter, Clare, was nine years old, my family stayed at a rustic bed and breakfast just outside Badlands National Park. Behind the lodge about a half mile away was a river so infused with white silt that the water in the river ran like milk. I found out later that the river is named the White River. Clare wanted to put her bare feet in the opaque water, so my wife, daughter, and I hiked down to the river one afternoon. I was worried about rattlesnakes, so I made sure everyone avoided the brush and stayed on the gravelly trail that led down to the river. That evening after dinner I was sitting on the back deck of the lodge, and I watched the owners of the bed and breakfast take a similar walk down to the water. Their three-old-son was running off-trail through some of the same terrain I'd forbidden Clare to go, and the parents were not concerned at all.

Maybe every region has an animal or two that worries outsiders, but is simply part of the landscape for the people who live there. The locals learn there are a few precautions to take, but otherwise the threatening reptile or large carnivore that unnerves visitors poses little actual danger. For me in the Great Lakes region of the Upper Midwest, the animal that most scares some nonresidents is the black bear.[1] I have friends from other parts of the country tell me they would never camp where there are bears. I suspect most of them underestimate the extensive natural range of black bears in North America, and I don't bother to correct them.

If I had to guess, I'd estimate I run into a black bear one backcountry trip in five. Yet when I do, unless the sighting is a fleeting glance, the event is memorable. Bear encounters are more about intensity than frequency. For example, in the September just prior to the COVID pandemic, three friends and I made our annual fishing trip to Canada's Lake of the Woods. Usually our trips coincided with the opening of walleye season in late May, but for the first time ever we went in the fall. I was excited for this change of seasons. In the past, September meant the start of a new school year, and I was not able to take any vacations when I had classes to teach. Now retired from the university, I looked forward to my first ever autumn fishing trip, as it promised fewer people, fewer bugs, cool air temperatures, and lake water that had had all summer to warm up before I jumped in for a bath. If I was lucky, even the leaves on the birch and aspen trees scattered among the evergreens would begin to show some color.

As has been the habit on our Canada trips, Clint, Tom, Jack, and I spent the first night at Clint's cabin on the lake's Snake Bay, then motored our fishing boats for two hours into the backcountry and set up camp on the westernmost point of a place called Deadbroke Island. The site has excellent sunsets and a small natural harbor just big enough for two boats. Jack once contacted the Lake of the Woods Museum in Kenora to ask about the history of the island's name. The museum staff could not report anything for certain, but told us that a failed 1890s goldmine on an adjacent island is known as the Dead Broke Occurrence. Which came first, the unsuccessful enterprise or the naming of the island, they could not say.

By late September the backcountry resorts were closed for the season, so we claimed sole possession of a thousand acres of islands and water. During the day we saw a few fishing boats other than our own, but by nightfall we enjoyed the illusion we were alone. Unfortunately the illusion was cut short. On the fourth day of our trip, a large houseboat entered our bay and tied up to shore about two hundred meters from our campsite. The houseboat towed three small V-hulls, and five fishermen used the smaller boats to fish during daylight hours and settled into the houseboat at night. A basic tenet of backcountry etiquette is to not set up camp near other people. With dozens of similar bays in the immediate area, it made no sense for them to anchor close to us.

Our frustration with the uninvited guests lessened when, on the second to the last evening of our trip, one of the guys in his small motorboat started yelling, "Hey, hey, hey!" At first, we thought he was yelling for one of his friends on the houseboat, so we ignored him. But as he drifted closer to our camp and kept yelling, we realized he was calling to us. We assumed he was having trouble with his outboard, so we walked over to the shoreline to see how we could help. He asked, "Did you fellas notice you have a bear in camp?" He pointed to the sandy isthmus connecting our small peninsula to the rest of the island. There sat a bear. It was looking directly at us, probably wondering whether it was safe to raid the kitchen. We had been eating dinner under a tarp when the guy in the boat had started yelling, and the smell of fried fish must have drawn in the bear.

We thanked the stranger, then banged on pans until the bear backed into the forest. A few minutes later it appeared on the shoreline halfway down the bay, and we realized we were dealing with two bears, not one. The bear that we'd seen on the isthmus stepped into the open and was immediately followed by a miniature version of herself. Our bear problem was a mom and her cub.

Bears are excellent swimmers, and it is a mistake to assume that camping on an island protects anyone from bears. Still, we thought our campsite was far enough from the mainland that a bear would not bother swimming out. Deadbroke Island itself is only about two kilometers long, but it is the westernmost link in a chain of islands. Our hope had been that the land mass of all of the islands combined would still be too small to serve as a home range for a bear. Obviously we were wrong.

Ordinarily when an area is known to have bears, best practice is to hang food from a tree overnight. Black bears climb trees, so the food has to be suspended from a rope tossed over a branch. The ideal branch is not easy to find. It should be narrow enough that a bear cannot crawl out on it to reach the rope. It should be well away from adjacent trees so the bear cannot approach the food from the side. The branch needs to be high enough that a food pack dangling below the branch is too far up for a bear to reach from the ground. Most of the trees near our camp were densely packed spruce, and none came close to working as an overnight pantry. Therefore, we had been leaving our food on the ground and hoping for the best. Now that we knew we had bears in the vicinity, we had no choice but to bear-proof our campsite. With no place to hang the food, we tossed it all into a boat, motored out to an exposed piece of granite in the middle of the lake, and left our food there for the night. It was far enough away from camp we doubted the bears would find it. Gulls might have a go at our pantry come morning, but we didn't think they had the strength or the smarts to break into our food bins.

I should point out that our usual party of four was down to three. Three days into our trip, Clint had taken one of two boats and headed back to civilization. His wife, Ellen, was at their cabin for a short vacation of her own. From the very start of our trip, Clint had planned to spend half of his vacation with his fishing buddies in the backcountry and half with Ellen at their cabin. Clint had been my tent partner. Once he left, I was alone in the tent nearest the kitchen. If the bears were to return, I was the first line of defense, so I took a metal pan and a big spoon to bed with me. Not much of an arsenal, but it was the only black bear deterrent I'd ever used.

The night was quiet with no bears. We retrieved our food from the little island before breakfast and correctly assumed it would be safe to leave it in camp during the day. The following evening, however, we decided to go back to our previous practice of leaving the food in camp. It was our last night before heading out, so even a successful raid by bears would only cost us the next morning's breakfast. The previous night when we'd taken our food cache out to the little island, wave action had slammed our boat against the rocks and put a ding in the prop. We didn't want to do more damage to our boat or our motor, so we went to bed with food in our kitchen area.

Shortly before dawn I heard what I initially thought was Tom or Jack rummaging through the kitchen to brew coffee. When the banging of a food container persisted, I realized something else was going on. I put on pants, grabbed my pan and spoon, and climbed out of my tent. Two days earlier I'd dropped and broken my only flashlight. When I looked in the direction of the kitchen, I couldn't see a thing—but the rummaging had stopped. My imagination got the better of me, and I thought I saw three dark forms that didn't belong there. As unlikely as it was that three bears would have teamed up for a predawn raid, I saw no reason to barge into the kitchen area for a better look. I stayed just outside my tent and banged my spoon and pan.

After what seemed liked nearly a minute of continuous banging by me, Jack and Tom in the tent away from the kitchen woke up and asked what was going on. Jack asked, "Steve, are you okay?" All I said was, "Bears in camp."

Once Tom and Jack emerged with their flashlights, we saw that it was the mom and her cub. The bears had pretty much ignored me when I was the only one trying to chase them away, but once Tom and Jack emerged, three men all yelling and clanking pans seemed to get them to move on. I finally went into the kitchen area to check out the damage. One food bin had been busted open, and a week's worth of trash was spread out over the ground. I started picking up the strewn garbage, when Jack walked over to me and said, "You know she's still right there." Jack shined his flashlight through the branches of a nearby shrub, and there sat the sow watching me from about fifteen feet away.

She had fooled me. I didn't know whether she wandered off with her cub and then circled back or if she never left in the first place—but there she was, barely outside the mess she'd created. She never threatened us, but in turn did not seem intimidated. We chased her and her cub away four or five times, and each time they lumbered back. No, more accurately I should state only the sow lumbered; the cub definitely had a bounce to its step. The pair finally left for good when Clint and Ellen showed up in their motorboat to help us break camp. Mama bear must have been impressed that we'd brought in reinforcements.

It was a series of small errors that led to the morning bear encounter. Most of my outdoor mishaps in recent years have been a result of multiple little mistakes rather than one big one. I consider myself fairly cautious in the backcountry. This has always been the case when I led organized groups, and it has become progressively more so even on my personal trips. Still, I get complacent when the consequences of ignoring common sense seem insignificant or unlikely to occur. My friends and I should have properly stored our food from day one. Failing to do so was wrong, but understandable. Not doing so after we saw bears in camp ranks high on the list of dumb things I've recently done in the backcountry. Secondly, we should have avoided aromatic meals, although there was no way we weren't going to fry fresh fish. Thirdly, we knew sows like to raise their cubs away from aggressive male bears, and we should have recognized Deadbroke Island as a potential nursery. Finally, the evidence of human presence in our campsite (e.g., a fire ring, trampled plant life, fish heads and bones tossed in the shallows offshore)[2] should have been a red flag. It meant that dozens of shore lunches had taken place at our campsite over the course of the summer—so even if we had kept an immaculate camp, the continuous flow of previous careless fishermen had attracted the bears and turned our campsite into a highlight of their nightly foraging routine.

Two days after we returned home from our fishing trip, Jack emailed everyone about something that had been on my mind as well. He'd spent an evening studying maps of Lake of the Woods and concluded it was time for us to venture deeper into the wilderness. We'd been displaced.

In recreation resource management vernacular, displacement is when a vacationer stops going to a particular destination because the destination has changed. It is usually when adventurers discover a new out-of-the-way place to visit. The most appealing aspect of the location is that it has no tourists and no tourist-related services. Then the word gets out, and less adventurous sightseers begin to show up. This leads to new hotels, restaurants serving nonlocal cuisine, tourist bars, and gift shops. The authenticity that attracted the original visitors no longer exists, so they stop coming. Eventually a tourism bureau materializes out of thin air and conducts a visitor survey. Everyone in the local tourism industry boasts that all of the visitors rate their experience as good or very good, but they fail to point out that the high satisfaction rate is due to the fact that the surveys were conducted after the displaced adventurers had long since moved on.[3]

Habituated bears and a lone houseboat do not fit the definition of mass tourism, but they were enough to disrupt a sense of untrammeled wilderness for our foursome. We had a good run, but now it was time to move on. Goodbye, Deadbroke Island.

14

Wisconsin West
Mark Twain on the Mekong

IN THE ESSAY "DEER SWATH," ALDO LEOPOLD DIVIDED OUTDOOR PEO-
ple into four categories.[1] He had deer hunters, duck hunters, bird hunters,
and nonhunters. Times have changed, and Leopold's classification system needs an update. Today slightly more than 4 percent of all Americans
hunt, which means Leopold's nonhunter classification takes in lots of different people doing lots of different things. If I was in charge of the re-
vision, I'd divide people by bodies of water. There would be lake people,
river people, ocean people, and waterless people. I was raised on a Great
Lake, had a brief and passionate love affair with the ocean, then settled
down in a river town only to discover I'd unknowingly been a river person all along.

The stories in this chapter are about the Mississippi River in relation to
two of her sister rivers in Asia. When I meet people in Taiwan, China, or
Southeast Asia for the first time, they always ask where I am from. They
know without asking that I am American, and there tends to be an assumption I'm either from California or the East Coast. When I tell them
I am from Wisconsin, there is almost always a blank reaction. When I

elaborate by telling them my home is along the Mississippi River, they then know where I live.

The Mississippi and the Yangtze

During most of my teaching career I did not work summers and was protective of my long summer breaks. For that reason, I hesitated when a friend at the US Geological Survey[2] asked me to host a visitor from China. My friend explained that Yang Xin (杨欣) was a noted environmentalist known for his photographs of the Tibetan Plateau. Mr. Yang wanted to write a series of magazine articles comparing life along the Upper Yangtze to that of the Upper Mississippi. My friend flattered me by saying that I, as a bit of a river rat, would be the perfect person to show the man around. When I asked whether Yang spoke English, I saw through the ruse. My friend needed someone—anyone—with a guest bedroom and a Mandarin-speaking spouse who could serve as interpreter.

After discussing the request with Manyu, we took in Yang Xin. La Crosse does not have much of an Asian community, so Manyu looks forward to having guests from China or Taiwan. From my perspective, I was treated so well when I taught in Asia that I welcome any opportunity to return the many kindnesses. Also, I thought comparing the upper stretches of the two countries' quintessential rivers was a good idea. I saw no downside to experiencing the Upper Mississippi through the eyes of a foreign visitor.

For two weeks during the summer of 2008, I was an Upper Mississippi River tour guide to the Chinese environmentalist. We paddled the backwaters. We watched barges pass through the lock and dam system. We hiked to the top of Brady's Bluff to get an aerial view of the river's wing dams. We observed white pelicans and bald eagles through spotting scopes. After the first two days, our routine evolved into Xin and me exploring the river during the day by ourselves, then joining Manyu for dinner and having her help us discuss all we had seen.

It was two seemingly inconsequential points of interest that left the biggest impression on our Chinese guest and, as a result, on me. The first was a trip to Goose Island County Park a few miles south of town. Goose Island was a place I often took students to canoe, but it is not a spot I'd ordinarily take a guest. Xin, however, wanted to photograph white-tailed deer, and Goose Island was the best place within a hundred miles to do that. It is now banned in the park, but until a few years ago, people dumped apples and old bread in a particular spot next to the park's main road. This makeshift feed lot attracted a variety of animals, and so long as a photographer kept the adjacent maintenance shed out of the shot, the habituated deer, raccoons, and crows passed as wild in a carefully cropped photograph.

Yang Xin took his deer photos, and as long as we were there, I showed him the rest of the park. Goose Island has boat landings, park shelters, hiking trails, and a campground. The campground does not have a maximum stay policy, so some people, mostly retirees, bring in mobile homes and live there for the entire summer. The concept of long-term camping was new to Xin. We drove through the campground late morning, and it was quiet but for one man driving around on a riding lawnmower. Yang Xin asked, "May we talk to the park worker?"

I told him in my clumsy Mandarin that we could ask, but should wait until he was done mowing. I also said, "I don't think he works here. I think he is a camper."

The man was tall, straight-backed, and in his mid-sixties. He mowed the campsites around three mobile homes, then parked his mower behind the middle trailer. I approached him, explained our purpose, and asked whether he'd answer a couple of questions. It turned out he was a park guest. He had a full-size refrigerator under an awning just outside the door of his mobile home, and as I would have expected, he reached inside the refrigerator, pulled out three Pabst Blue Ribbons, and invited us to join him at his picnic table.

Xin asked me simple questions in Mandarin, and I repeated them in English. Mostly he wanted to know how long the man camped in the park and why the man valued the river so much. Xin then wanted to know where the man was from.

After I translated the question for the man, he answered, "La Crosse."

Xin did not wait for me to respond back to him in Mandarin, but instead immediately said, "No, I know we are in La Crosse. I want to know where the man lives during the rest of the year."

"The man is from La Crosse," I said. Xin did not believe me, and he asked me to ask the man again.

"Yeah," the man replied to my follow-up question. "Lived in La Crosse my whole life. My house is only three miles northeast of here. My wife will join me for dinner, but she won't stay the night. She thinks I'm crazy for spending summers here, but she also looks forward to her time with me gone. Sometime this summer we'll take a trip to the Black Hills and stay in a motel, but that's her vacation, not mine. I'd rather be right here."

I couldn't translate the man's response into Mandarin, so I said, "His home is in La Crosse. I'll explain it better when we get back with Manyu."

"Good," said Xin, "because this does not make any sense to me."

The second noteworthy stop was the national fish hatchery near the town of Genoa. The hatchery office and the artificial ponds are on opposite sides of Highway 35 from each other, so it is not uncommon for the pond side of the hatchery to feel deserted. I parked the car, and we walked the grounds on our own. The area has a dozen outdoor ponds plus a series of buildings with tanks inside. On the day we visited, several of the ponds had been drained, so we wandered from building to building to look inside.

The first building had tanks filled with small clams. I did not know the Chinese words for "invasive species" or "clam," but I did my best to explain that invasive clams and mussels had reduced the population of native clams in the Upper Mississippi. The hatchery was trying to replenish the native stock. I also reminded myself to ask Manyu to tell Xin that one of the early industries of La Crosse was mother of pearl buttons made from freshwater clamshells.

We then wandered into a second building and found three tanks containing young lake sturgeon. Even before Xin could ask, I told him that I did not know what the sturgeon were for. Fortunately a hatchery worker walked into the building as we were getting ready to leave. He explained that federal hatcheries, unlike state facilities, have to earn their keep. If they don't generate enough funding through grants and contracts, they close down. They are, in effect, hatcheries for hire. The sturgeon were a contract with the Bad River Indian Reservation in northern Wisconsin. An Ojibwe tradition is to spear Lake Superior sturgeon as they enter rivers to spawn, but dams, overfishing, and habitat destruction had decimated the numbers. The tribe had hired the hatchery to restock sturgeon in the rivers along the lake's southern shore.

The hatchery worker told the whole story without interruption, so Xin went nearly five minutes without knowing what the guy was saying. Even after the man finished talking, I could only explain to Xin that the story was too complicated for me to translate, but that it was a good story. We would talk about it when we got back together with Manyu. Both Xin and I thanked the hatchery worker, and we drove back to La Crosse.

At dinner that night, I repeated the sturgeon story to Manyu, and she retold it in Mandarin. Xin had never heard of a government agency helping indigenous people maintain their traditions. The Chinese government was so determined to destroy Tibetan culture on the Tibetan Plateau that it had not occurred to him that the opposite was even possible. I asked Manyu to tell him that my government's record toward native peoples was not very good. Xin smiled and, in carefully worded Mandarin I could understand, said, "Everybody knows that."

The Yangtze and the Min

Two years after Yang Xin's trip to La Crosse, Manyu and I visited him in Chengdu, and I had my own river revelation. Chengdu is near the confluence of the Minjiang (Min River) and Upper Yangtze. An irrigation system on the Minjiang, at a place called Dujiangyan, is one of the engineering wonders of the ancient world.[3] The Minjiang flows rapidly as it comes off the Tibetan Plateau, then slows abruptly when it reaches the flatlands outside of Chengdu. The change in water speed silts up the main channel and causes annual flooding. To address the problem, Chinese engineers in the third century BCE built a series of levees, spillways, and canals to regulate the flow of water. The wonder of the system is that it is done without a dam or mechanical device. In the springtime, most of the water flows through a deep and narrow outer channel away from major human development. Even if there is flooding, the damage is minimal. During the rest of the year, water flows through a shallower inner channel that serves a large irrigation system. A pair of levees, one as big as an island, somehow gets the water to naturally shift its course depending on the flow and water level. Equally important, the levees cause the water in the outer channel to swirl, and this spinning action is enough to pick up the silt and disperse it across a greater distance. The original design (no longer in use) included rocks inside huge underwater wicker baskets that could be dismantled and reassembled as needed. Whereas most modern dams are cursed by siltation, the ancient Dujiangyan system actually removes silt as part of its design.

I thought back to the afternoon on Brady's Bluff when I tried to explain the simple beauty of the wing dams on the Mississippi River. Wing dams are angled piles of rock that extend from both shorelines of the river. These mini dams deflect the natural water flow toward the center of the river, and the increased volume in the center then washes silt out of the navigation channel. When I showed the wing dams to Xin, he had to be thinking, "Yeah, my culture has something similar, but we did it better and we did it twenty-three hundred years ago."

Once I returned to La Crosse after the Chengdu visit, I searched for information to better understand the hydraulics of the Dujiangyan levees. I failed at that, but in the process learned that the Dujiangyan area is also a place of religious and philosophical significance. Nearby Mount Qingcheng was the refuge of first-century hermit Zhang Lin (張陵), one of the fathers of Taoism. I was a little disappointed that Yang Xin had not told me about the significance of Mount Qingcheng when I was in Chengdu. Still, the belated information reminded me of a passage from

Walden. Thoreau had studied the *Bhagavad Gita* during his two years at Walden Pond and described his research as "the pure Walden Pond [mingling with] the sacred water of the Ganges."[4] The Yangtze is not the Ganges, nor is the Tao Hinduism, but I see parallels between Thoreau's experience and my own. I feel that I too have mingled two great waters. How often do I get to do that?

Unexpectedly, the answer to this rhetorical question is *twice.* A dozen years ago I mixed the Mississippi River with the Yangtze. More recently I blended it with the Mekong.

The Mississippi and the Mekong

Whenever I travel for more than a week at a time, I take with me a paperback classic that, for whatever reason, I haven't read at home. For a recent trip to southern Laos, I took *A Connecticut Yankee in King Arthur's Court.*[5] I grabbed it almost as an afterthought. It is not one of Mark Twain's best books, but was one of only a few by him I hadn't already read. As a result, I found myself under a thatched roof next to the Mekong River reading a book by the novelist who personifies a river half a world away.

The protagonist in *A Connecticut Yankee* is knocked unconscious by a hit on the head and wakes up in sixth-century Camelot. My own trip to Laos also felt a bit like time travel into a past era. Only a week earlier I had been ice fishing on a Mississippi River backwater in Wisconsin, and now I was in the Laotian tropics during its dry season. In several ways, I was as disoriented as the hero in Twain's novel. The area in Laos I visited was rural and largely undeveloped. I couldn't communicate with the locals, I seldom knew where I was in relation to anywhere else, and I was having a hard time converting US dollars into Laotian kip.[6] Except for the fact that the Lao language is similar to Thai and two of my traveling companions, my sister-in-law and her husband, spoke Thai, I would have never gotten into Laos at all. Manyu had some problems with her Taiwanese passport at the Thai–Lao border, and without Manyu's sister's ability to speak to the Laotian border officials, we would have been turned away before we even got started.

We visited several places in Southern Laos,[7] but our best lodging was in the village of Champasak. The condition of the guesthouse was actually more run-down than some of the other places we stayed, but its shortcomings were offset by the fact that it was located right on the banks of the Mekong River. Every morning I woke up before everyone else in my traveling party and sat at river's edge with my book. I read a little, drank the local coffee until my hands trembled, and watched the river. The water in the Mekong looked exactly like the water in the Mississippi—muddy, wide, and with enough current I didn't want to fall in accidentally. Little else, however, was the same. The vegetation on the banks was dominated by bamboo and coconut palms. The birds were a tad more colorful. The boats on the water were not like anything I'd ever seen in the US. They were more reminiscent of the water taxis that dominate the khlongs in Bangkok.

The boats were long and skinny watercraft called three-plank boats, so named because their unique design consists of a wide plank for the floor with two narrower planks making up the sides. The floor plank is warped upward both bow and stern to create the hull. Sizes of the boats varied, but the most common were twenty feet long and no more than four feet wide. I saw a few men poling their boats, but the majority were powered by long-tailed[8] outboard motors. As far as I could tell, the boats were used to transport people, haul small cargo, provide recreation, and work fishing nets. During my first Champasak morning, I watched men and boys put out nets in the river and wondered why they hadn't left them out all night. That evening I realized that limited boat traffic continued throughout the night, but was done without lights. Any nets left in the river would have been caught up in someone else's prop. The river, at least along this section, was the major thoroughfare for the community, and the people in the village were as comfortable on the water as on land.

When I observe people in non-North American cultures interact with nature, I wonder about its effect on my own relationship with nature. I don't think it affects it much. Even though I believe my informal study of Tao philosophy has significantly changed the way I look upon the natural world, observing people in Taiwan, China, and Southeast Asia has not. I notice similarities and differences between their interactions and my own, but if those observations have redirected my thinking in any way, I am not recognizing it.

For example, my entourage on the Laotian trip, which consisted of my wife, my mother-in-law, my wife's sisters, and the husbands of my wife's sisters, chartered a van during our visit. We were on the wrong side of the river when we first headed for Champasak. At one point, we were only five kilometers from the village, but seventy kilometers from the nearest bridge. On the sections of the Mekong that serve as the border between Thailand and Laos, bridges are almost nonexistent. Even when both sides of the river are in Laos, which is the case at Champasak, the situation improves only slightly. When we were on the wrong side of the river, we could almost smell catfish cooking at the Champasak riverside restaurants,[9] but still had what I thought was a long drive ahead of us. The nearest bridge was over an hour away in the city of Pakse, so a round trip to the bridge and back was going take the better part of the afternoon.

In retrospect, I realized it was narrow-minded of me to think there was only one way to cross a river with a twelve-passenger van. Without warning, our Laotian driver turned off the main road, bumped two kilometers down a pair of sandy ruts and then gunned the van up a ramp of parallel two-by-twelves onto a rickety wooden platform lashed atop a trio of welded-together Vietnam War–era gunboat hulls. We were to ferry across. Hank Morgan, the main character in *A Connecticut Yankee in King Arthur's Court*, would have been impressed by the unique design of our transport, but I was not. Except for the fact that the Rube Goldberg contraption was powered by a propeller attached to an automobile engine, I'm not sure its construction was anything different from what the Connecticut Yankee might have experienced in crossing the Thames. Everyone from Manyu's side of the family marveled at the novelty of the crossing. I, on the other hand, was nervous and spent most of the boat ride trying to recall which of my in-laws couldn't swim, so I'd know which ones to grab when the whole thing capsized. We made the crossing without incident.

One of my most interesting observations of the local people interacting with the Mekong River was not at Champasak, but downstream at Khone Falls. A sign for visitors at the falls (it might have been the only sign anywhere on the river written in both Lao and English) described Khone Pha Pheng Falls as the largest waterfalls in the world. I didn't believe the claim, but nonetheless enjoyed the massive amount of water cascading through a series of craggy rapids. When I got home, I googled the Mekong and learned that Khone Falls, from bank to opposite bank, is the widest waterfalls in the world—so by one measure it is the biggest. Khone Falls is a formidable barrier, and it is the only reason commercial traffic on the Mekong does not extend all the way from the Pacific Ocean to China. The falls are, in terms of a natural barrier, the Niagara Falls of the Mekong, and I suspect the day will come when Laos (with Chinese funding) will compromise the ecology of the river's upper regions by building a lock and dam system not unlike the St. Lawrence's Welland Canal. Such a structure would enhance commerce in Southeast Asia and southern China, but simultaneously provide a convenient thoroughfare for invasive aquatic species.

At Khone Falls, I watched three couples catching fish alongside the wildest sections of the falls. The men each held a two-foot piece of small-gauge netting stretched between a pair of sticks. Had they lowered their nets directly into the torrent, the raging rapids would either have ripped the nets from their hands or pulled both the nets and the men into the river. Instead of placing the nets in the water, the men held them about a foot above it. Every thirty seconds or so flat roundish fish the size of a lemon slice would be tossed into the air, and the men would catch them in their nets. They'd immediately bag the small fish, and after collecting a dozen or so, the men handed the bag off to the women. The women would then climb the rocks until they were beyond the mist of the rapids and lay the fish out in the sun to dry. The fish had silvery sides similar to herring, so they glistened like little mirrors. From where I stood and watched, these people were putting themselves in peril just to net little medallions of fish jerky. I had to assume that the perceived risk was greater than the actual danger—and these local river people knew exactly what they were doing.

One evening in Champasak, Manyu's family and I had dinner with the princess of Laos. I don't know all of the details of how we came to have dinner with royalty, but the princess had fled to France as a young woman when the Communists took over. When she had been allowed to return decades later, my French brother-in-law, Yves, had somehow helped the princess and her French husband settle back in, and they had become friends. At dinner, the princess's husband explained to Yves and me that he was trying to find investors to build a small wharf in Champasak. Three sites with twelfth-century Khmer ruins were currently being unearthed just outside of the village, and Champasak now had potential as a tourist destination. A sticking point, however, was that the town needed a place for tour boats from Pakse to dock. The princess's husband wanted to make sure the waterfront development, which he considered inevitable, was done in a way that would benefit the locals as much as it would the outside tour operators.

When I walked the streets of Champasak, children ran up to me. They did not beg, nor did they try to sell me trinkets. They just gawked, waved, and laughed. Yves explained that these kids were familiar with young French and German travelers, but I might have been their first sighting of an old Westerner with a full Santa Claus beard. As far as I am concerned, being seen as an oddity by the locals is always a good sign. While I believe the intentions of the princess's husband are honorable and he has no interest in personally lining his pockets from an enhanced tourist trade, part of me hopes all efforts toward a wharf project fail. Tourism, even ecotourism, is always a two-edged sword. Regardless of what the big money says, no one ever really knows whether the positives of tourism outweigh the negatives until the whole thing is a done deal.

15

Wisconsin West
What About the Other Kids?

WHEN CLARE WAS IN ELEMENTARY SCHOOL, MEMBERS OF MY CHURCH asked me to lead a series of outdoor excursions for families in the congregation. My own attempts at linking nature to Christianity have been disappointing, but I could not, in good conscience, ignore an effort to get fellow parishioners out of their man-made sanctuary into a natural one. For one of our outings, we took a hike along the banks of the East Fork of the Black River. An hour and a half's drive northeast of La Crosse, the scenic river from the town of Pray all the way to its mouth at Lake Arbutus forms the northern border of the Black River State Forest. I knew the East Fork well because I often paddle it in the spring, but I'd never hiked the trail that ran parallel to the river. Also, I'd never been to that section of the Black River at that time of year. This was August, and by June the river runs too shallow to canoe or kayak. Still, I often saw others on the trail when I was paddling, and it seemed an easy and pretty route.

Much of the established path runs atop a steep embankment. The elevated perspective provides an excellent view of the river, but was a frustration for the kids on the hike. For them, they could see the water, but not get to it. When the trail eventually dropped down to river's edge, the kids shot for the water like retrievers out of a duck blind. The river was seasonally low, and dozens of ottoman-sized boulders poked out of the tannin-stained water that gives the Black River its name. Immediately the kids started jumping from rock to rock to see if they could get all the way across without getting their feet wet.

Immediately one of the parents shouted, "Get back here now! You're going to fall in the river."

The overly protective parent was right, at least in terms of someone falling in. Three of the kids were moving so tentatively they were in no danger of a misstep. The rest, however, about a dozen in total, were fearless. It was only a matter of time before one of them miscalculated and fell, and my guess was that as soon as one kid went into the water by accident, the rest were going in on purpose. Having said that, if ever a river had been made to fall into, it was the East Fork of the Black River that August afternoon. The weather was warm, the sun was out, the current was slow, and the water was less than a foot deep in most places. Most of the kids obediently returned to shore. Clare, already midstream, did not. She spun around on the rock where she was standing and scoured the shoreline for me among the parents. When our eyes met, she gave me a look that said, "What the hell?" Clare did not swear when she was eight years old and, to this day, does not swear in my presence, but I don't know how better to describe her facial expression and body language.

I waved for Clare to come in, and when she reached me, I quietly promised we would come back later to play in the river. She whispered back, "Yeah, but what about the other kids?"

Had my mind been a little sharper, I would have immediately recognized the insight in Clare's words. Instead, I did not appreciate their full implication until a month later in my autumn outdoor recreation course at the university. My students and I were discussing Richard Louv's *Last Child in the Woods*.[1] I'd intentionally chosen the book as required reading because I was sure the students would find fault with Louv's basic premise. In the book, he claimed that baby boomers were the last generation where children were afforded unsupervised and unstructured time in nature—and therefore, were the last generation to have a strong personal relationship with the natural world.

Most of the students in my outdoor recreation courses were either farm kids surrounded by acres of farmland or townies from communities small enough to have large undeveloped tracts a short bicycle ride away. I expected them to dismiss Louv as a big city journalist from the West Coast who had no concept of life in the Upper Midwest.

I was wrong. The students agreed with Louv on this point right down to his last semicolon. They all believed Louv's description of their millennial generation was accurate—but that they, as college students majoring in outdoor recreation, were exceptions to the rule. They considered themselves environmental anomalies and used the nearby La Crosse River Marsh to make their case, pointing out that an intriguing natural resource was only three blocks from campus, yet many of their fellow students had never set foot there.

I was faced with the realization that my environmental education work, whether it was with my daughter or with my students, had evolved into preaching to the choir. When I was confronted by a worried church parent along the Black River, I froze and allowed one cautious person to suck the fun out of the best part of the day. I'd forgotten such nervous Nellies actually existed.

There was a time when I taught students who came to me without nature already preprogrammed into their hearts. On my hikes with sixth graders in Northern California, for example, the redwoods sometimes were the kids' first introduction to the outdoors. Only after I began teaching college students majoring in outdoor recreation did my work transition from introducing novices to nature to training experienced people for careers in the outdoors. Aldo Leopold, in my favorite Leopold essay that is not part of *A Sand County Almanac*, wrote on this very subject, and I can only assume that he too was confronted with this same situation in his own university teaching. In "The Role of Wildlife in a Liberal Education," he lamented that higher education has an "obvious preference for preparing [students] to earn a salary rather than to live a life." Leopold took the contemporary debate of liberal arts education versus career preparation and directed it specifically at the professional training in outdoor recreation and resource management. He felt professors who did a good job of preparing outdoor professionals often did a poor job of educating the student body as a whole.

The two main points of his essay are (1) higher education's most concerted efforts now are directed toward professional training rather than a liberal arts education and (2) even when nature-related educators offer an introductory course for nonmajors, they tend to provide a watered-down version of a professional preparation course, not the entirely different course that would better serve the students. As Leopold stated it:

> Liberal education in wildlife is not merely a diluted dosage of technical education. It calls for somewhat different teaching materials and sometimes even different teachers. The objective is to teach the student to see the land, to understand what he sees, and enjoy what he understands. I say land rather than wildlife, because wildlife cannot be understood without understanding the landscape as a whole. Such teaching could well be called land ecology rather than wildlife, and could serve very broad educational purposes.[2]

The general education courses Leopold called for, if they ever existed in the first place, have become a rarity at publicly funded universities. Fiscally minded administrators see general education as tuition generators and favor the kind of survey courses that jam hundreds of students into a large auditorium at very little cost.[3] Intimate introductory courses, such as those that might include field trips to natural areas, are mostly gone, and it is no wonder students see general education requirements as a boring obstacle to degree completion. As soon as a physical education department, an art department, a biology department, or an outdoor recreation program loses a faculty member due to budget cuts, some of the first courses to be eliminated are labor-intensive outdoor courses for nonmajors. Department chairs have no choice but to put the needs of their own declared majors over the needs of the student body as a whole, and service courses for inquisitive nonmajors become expendable. The pattern is this: First, due to a temporary reduction in teaching staff, the introductory survey course is not offered for one semester. Then it is dropped for a year or two. Eventually, when it becomes obvious the cut in staffing is going to be permanent, the course is deleted from the course catalog — and once it is gone from the catalog, the next batch of first-year students doesn't even know the course ever existed. At public universities, a true liberal arts education is becoming progressively more difficult to obtain — and the only students with a true appreciation of nature tend to be those who possessed it before they ever stepped foot on campus.[4]

Even though the students in my class agreed with Richard Louv that most people their age lacked a personal connection with nature, they disagreed with him when he wrote that the solution was unsupervised childhood play. When I asked them to describe the specific unsupervised experiences that helped them to foster their love of nature, the consensus was that by the time they were old enough to play in nature without an adult looking over their shoulders, their link to the natural world had already been established. In their minds, personal relationships with nature do not come from unsupervised time in nature, but from unstructured outdoor experiences with their parents. All of them played in nature without adults by the time they were seven or eight years old, but impressionable encounters with nature went back even further, went back as far back as they could remember. As one student put it, his very earliest recollections, now not much more than vague impressions on the very edge of his long-term memory, included lakes, woods, beaches, and family. As a parent who hikes and paddles with his own daughter, I was touched by the way these young adults spoke affectionately about their moms and dads when it came to the outdoors. For these students, there was a direct and obvious correlation between their love of nature and the parents who took them hunting, fishing, camping, hiking, birdwatching, morel-picking, cross-country skiing, canoeing, and gardening.[5]

Weed Wrenches

Since the birth of my daughter, my environmental education efforts have fallen into the two distinct categories described above. There is my professional work with college students and my role as a parent. Only once do I remember these two spheres intersecting, and oddly it was at a time when I wasn't teaching college students at all. I was nearing the end of my academic career. I'd just shifted primarily to an administrative position at my university, and I taught very little. This transition to administration often is known as going over to the dark side, and the teacher in me does not disagree.

It was a Saturday in early October. I remember fall colors seemed late that year, and only the sumac and an odd tree here and there had turned. Clare and I were hiking in the US Fish and Wildlife Service's Trempealeau National Wildlife Refuge when we bumped into a group of students from a university class that, only a few semesters earlier, would have been mine. The students were using weed wrenches to remove buckthorn and Chinese elm from a large restored prairie. Weed wrenches are hybrid hand tools, part oversized Vise-Grips and part five-foot-long pry bar, that, when clamped to the very base of a woody invasive plant, can be used to pull the plant out by its roots. Use of the tool, to some extent, doubles as a team-building exercise, because there is a trick to the extraction. Too little pressure and nothing moves. Too much pressure applied abruptly snaps the taproot. Only a slow steady pull by three or four students working on the weed wrench in unison gets the entire plant out. Two people were in charge. One was a professor I'd helped to hire and the other was the refuge naturalist, a woman I'd worked with in the past. I stopped to talk. When I noticed Clare looking longingly at the conservation work, I asked the coleaders and the students if they would mind if Clare helped. They all invited her to join in, and as I would have expected, the good-hearted outdoor recreation majors immediately accepted her as a little sister.

In jeans and a light autumn jacket, Clare, even at age fourteen, was barely distinguishable from the college students. Still, my strongest sense as I witnessed my professional and personal worlds converge was that Clare was having a different experience than the students—this, in spite of that fact that she was in the same place at the same time doing the same thing. With Clare, everything had been unstructured, and she was benefiting from the spontaneity of the day. As with nearly all of our nature outings, we'd come to the refuge with no specific plans in mind. Maybe something memorable would happen, but if not, that was fine. On this particular day, Clare was being treated as an equal by a group of college students. For a high school freshman, that is memorable.

My sense was that it was not the same for the college students. Unless Laurie Harmon, the new instructor, had significantly revised the way I'd originally designed the course, there was not a great deal of spontaneity in the outing. Even use of the weed wrenches was part of an orchestrated day designed to meet specific predetermined learning outcomes. The students knew exactly what to expect before they arrived at the refuge. Removing invasive species was a planned activity within the much broader context of recreation resource management. The students were supposed to have read beforehand short essays about prairie restoration and about the major invasive plant species of the Upper Midwest. Jenny Lilla, the refuge naturalist, had explained to them the history of the Trempealeau National Wildlife Refuge,[6] and Laurie had lectured them about the US Fish and Wildlife Service's unique niche within the various state and federal resource management agencies. Depending on how carefully Laurie had followed my old syllabus, the students may even have had a lesson on the effective use of volunteers on public lands. The irony is that by consciously arming the students with pertinent information prior to the trip, some of the magic that comes with "just going to nature to see what happens" was lost.

Kenneth Boulding[7] wrote that formal education impacts students in one of three ways. Way one is in one ear and out the other. No teacher wants this result, but knows it sometimes happens. Way two is incremental impact. Education aims to tweak student perceptions by small degrees. For example, some of the students who worked the weed wrenches may not have known prior to their outing the difference between a prairie and a fallow farm field, but now, because of readings, lectures, and fieldwork, they did. Finally, way three is an impact that reaches students at their core and decidedly changes their lives from that point on.

Most teachers, myself included, focus on way two, the incremental change. We strive to bring all students up to a minimum level of competence on a particular subject. Even though many teach because of the handful of times they significantly change students' lives, results of this magnitude are unusual and not part of day-to-day instruction. In an educational system of large class sizes, predetermined learning outcomes, and constant assessment of both student and teacher, formal education is more about impacting *all* students a little bit and less about reaching one or two students at a deeper level.

With teaching someone's own child, however, the reverse is true. As Clare's dad, I was her private tutor. When I was with my daughter, I had the luxury and joy of going all in with each nature outing. I rarely thought about affecting incremental change. I only cared that Clare learned to love wild things. I was more concerned about her heart and her gut than her brain. Of course, ecological content was introduced when it seemed appropriate, but factoids were only supplemental to the more grandiose purposes of our short excursions.

I hope I am right in thinking that the hit-and-miss approach I took with my daughter would not have worked well with students who were with me for only a few hours a week over a period of a single semester. Throughout Clare's young life, she and I have gone to the Trempealeau National Wildlife Refuge twenty or thirty times. With those visits, most had been pleasant, but not eventful. Mixed in with the commonplace, however, were times when Clare held and banded a northern waterthrush, observed white pelicans corral and feed on bait fish, counted the number of spawning carp piled up against the lower side of a spillway, collected fresh lotus seeds for her mom's Asian cooking, and was chased by a northern water snake in her kayak. None of these special moments were planned. Even the bird banding, which could have been arranged ahead of time, was a matter of the right place at the right time. I know these events have left an impression on Clare, because often during recent trips to the refuge, Clare breaks the silence of our walks to say, "Dad, remember that time we . . . ?"

One time Clare asked, "Dad, remember that time we walked the dike and saw all of those bullhead heads on the ground?" I remembered the outing, but hadn't thought about it until Clare brought it up. It was an indication that Clare's memorable moments may not be the same as mine. Clare had to remind me that we'd seen over a dozen decapitated fish heads on the dike, but didn't know what had put them there. We went to the refuge office afterward to ask Jenny about the heads, but she was off that day. The person in the office guessed that the bullhead heads had been left by fish-eating birds, maybe terns that had somehow detached the heads as a way to avoid swallowing the sharp spines on the bullheads' pectoral fins.

Clare's visits to the refuge are in contrast to my trips with college students. I held class at the refuge once or twice a year for twenty years, but it was always with a different group of students. Each student went there with me only once. On one particular outing, students and I did see pelicans so thick that it was wall-to-wall white feathers. Another time we did help with bird banding just as Clare had. I took advantage of these teachable moments when they popped up, but remarkable opportunities happened maybe five or six times total. If I intentionally took students to the refuge with no plans and only hopes that something exceptional would happen, the most likely result would be a pleasant walk without a significant occurrence. Conversely, with a set agenda and orchestrated activities, I was guaranteed incremental changes in the students' understanding of the natural world. In other words, I went to the refuge with Clare dozens of times and waited for the spectacular to take place. I went there with my students only once and organized the trip so at least something small, something relatively interesting, was sure to occur.

Some parents are hesitant to be environmental educators with their kids because they lack ecological knowledge. If family outings had to be fact-driven, this might make sense. But because the goals should be grander and not particularly scientific, it should not matter whether parents know the difference between a mayfly and a June bug. A parent needs to know only enough to make time in nature fun. The great moments in nature do not need interpretation, but they do need time. Unless parents become the main providers of frequent outings in nature, young kids won't get to visit natural areas often enough for the rare and exceptional moments to occur. And if young kids don't have exceptional moments in nature with their parents, they might not get excited about nature later in life.

Dan Egan, author of *The Death and Life of the Great Lakes*, was asked what the general population could do to help save the Great Lakes from ecological disaster.[8] His answer was to take their kids to play along the beach on the Great Lakes. The next generation, he claimed, will take the resource for granted unless it is an important part of its childhood.

Wisconsin has been the bookends to my life, at least my life until this point. I grew up here, left for twenty years, and now have returned. Certainly one of the biggest rewards of returning to Wisconsin has been playing with Clare in the same kinds of ecosystems as those that shaped my life. She and I could have hiked and canoed almost anywhere, but I cannot think of many things better than reliving my own childhood while introducing nature to my daughter. The door to a solid environmental ethic is never closed, but it is open the widest when a child's daily life revolves around his or her parents. That does not mean, of course, that the rest of us should stop trying to expose people to nature once they get older. For all I know, the weed wrench experience in the Trempealeau National Wildlife Refuge was a significant memory for someone besides Clare.

Environmental educators who have students for only a short period of time plan for incremental change, but hope for something more. It's an odd way of doing things, but I'm not sure how else it can be.

16

Three Outsdoorsmen and a Philosopher

THREE OUTDOORSMEN AND A PHILOSOPHER WALK INTO A BAR. THERE is no punchline here. It's just what happened. It was late afternoon just after work, and I was one of the outdoorsmen. Two of the men briefly disagreed on the attributes of a couple of craft beers and then ordered a local IPA. With a full pitcher, four glasses, and a basket of unshelled peanuts, we sat down at a small table in the back room.

I started the conversation. "I've been thinking about unusual experiences in nature. My theory is that the more time we spend in nature the more likely we are to pile up experiences that happen once and only once—and these unique events contribute to our relationship with the natural world. So I have a question for you. If I say once-in-a-lifetime experience in nature, what memory pops into your head? Don't analyze the question. Just tell me the first thing that comes to mind."

Richard, easily the most talkative of the group and one of the outdoorsmen, wanted to go first. "It was in high school," he said. "I was sitting alone on the edge of the marsh here in town. For English class we were reading *Walden*, and I was enamored with the book and the place that Thoreau was describing. It took me almost fifty years, but I finally visited Walden Pond two summers ago. And it all started with reading

Thoreau in the marsh. For the first time ever, I realized literature had the power to touch my real life."

Buzz, the outdoorsman other than Richard and me, went next. "I was squirrel hunting with my dad out near Necedah. I was probably fourteen years old. After my dad parked the car, we took off in opposite directions. We carried food for lunch and stayed out for the day. I remember that the morning started out still, then a breeze developed at midday. I watched white clouds slowly move into an otherwise blue sky. About an hour before sunset, the wind stopped altogether, and it was time to return to the car. On the walk out of the woods I realized this was what living was supposed to be."

Finally Sam, the philosopher, spoke. Sam does not spend as much time in the woods as either Richard or Buzz, but he likes to hike and camp with his family and is more outdoorsy than a stereotypical philosophy professor. He said, "I was a military brat, and I lived in Italy for a couple of years. I liked to leave the base and wander through the Italian countryside. Usually I found a tree to read in. I didn't speak Italian, and the local farmers didn't speak English. Still, they were always kind to me. I think the strange American kid amused them. No specific day stands out, but all of my time spent reading in Italy is really important to me."

I did not tell my friends that their answers weren't what I was looking for. I wasn't expecting ascents of K2, but I was hoping for events that were at least out of the ordinary. Instead, two of them talked about reading books and a third about watching clouds. Where was the once-in-a-lifetime part in any of these stories? Wasn't there an incident where a tree fell on one of their tents and nearly killed them? Didn't they ever see ocean waves glow in the dark? Didn't they ever have a trail blocked by a bear or a rattlesnake or maybe even a pile of elephant dung?[1]

The problem, of course, was my expectation and not their interpretation of my question. In their minds, they were conveying events that were once in a lifetime. One had discovered that literature can touch the soul. Another had, for at least a short time, understood the meaning of life. A third had wandered the Italian countryside as a young boy. How much more was I looking for? I'd already learned from students and my daughter that no one can really understand which events in nature will touch another person. Why was I expecting something different from my friends?

The first rule of competent research is to go in with an open mind, and I hadn't done that. Instead I'd tracked down a few like-minded friends (another violation of good research methodology) and expected them to confirm my hypothesis that a series of spectacular moments cements a bond with nature. Fortunately my friends set me straight and reminded me that the spectacular is only the tip of the iceberg when it comes to meaningful experiences in the natural world. Apparently I hadn't been paying close enough attention to my own recollections. Didn't I remember that a brief sighting of a pileated woodpecker left a lasting impression? Hadn't I discovered during a drive home from Leopold's Shack that the reflection of an event may be as important as the event itself? Hadn't I gone so far as to suggest, in recalling an encounter with an otter, that adults miss out on once-in-a-lifetime moments by making too much of them?

Still, the barroom discussion did nothing to dissuade me from wanting to explicitly identify at least a few common elements that make occurrences in nature special. To conclude that every moment in nature has the potential to be special serves no useful purpose. It is just as pointless as the inane supposition that all education is environmental education. Both statements are too general to be of any use. They offer no guidance for how an educator might proceed. If all education was environmental, then there would be no reason to offer curriculum specifically identified as such. If all moments in nature have equal potential to be personally significant, then there is no reason to take steps to enhance the chances for magic.

I have come up with a few assumptions about special moments in nature. They are imprecise. They tend to point out the obvious. They work around the edges rather than go to the heart of things. They are, however, the best that I can do.

Meaningful activities in nature require going out into nature.

I lived in Boston during the Great Blizzard of 1978. It was the only time in my life nature was so bold as to come to me rather than the other way around. The city shut down, and driving personal vehicles was banned. People walked or skied down the middle of streets. It was the best two weeks of my three years in Massachusetts. I suppose that, in addition to the Great Blizzard, I've also had a few moments when the wild was witnessed from the comfort of my house. Through my living room window I've seen a Cooper's hawk take down a starling. From the back stoop I've watched cedar waxwings passing hackberries to each other as they sat in a row on a branch. Still, the best opportunities for special moments happen when I leave the house, leave the neighborhood, and immerse myself in a woods or a river or a marsh (or a mountain or a shoreline or a desert...). All of us need to get out.

Defining moments in nature include grandiose events in exotic places, but there are also small treasures that happen in the natural areas near home.

The Yosemites of the world are conducive to special moments. Spectacular places make for spectacular experiences. That being said, I have been to Yosemite once, the Grand Canyon once, and I've never been to Yellowstone. If I waited for exceptional locations for magical moments, my list would not be very long. In contrast to my occasional visits to the great national parks, I've been to the marsh near my home up to a hundred times a year for the past twenty-five years. I never go there expecting something special to happen, but occasionally it does. It's an ecologically rich place. Yosemite has the advantage that even an inattentive visitor will see the specialness. The beauty of a local marsh is more subtle, but there are special moments to be had through an open mind, a little bit of patience, and multiple visits.

Nothing in a memorable experience needs to be difficult or arduous.

When I think about my notable times in nature, there is not a *Heart of Darkness* adventure among them. I would have been thrilled had there been, but my most vivid recollections of events with nature are of the woodpecker-in-the-front-yard variety. Ninety-five percent of my time in nature has been within a day's drive of wherever I was living at the time, and most of my memorable experiences have been within twenty miles of a trailhead or canoe landing. I am fairly sure that well over half of most people's special moments in nature have been within a few hours of home.

Magic in nature is unexpected.

The funniest jokes are those where the punch line comes out of nowhere, and the most pleasant moments in nature are a surprise. When I was in my early twenties, I boarded a tour boat in Acadia National Park to see seals. The highlight of the trip was when a large bird flew over the bow. I instinctively shouted, "What was that?" It was the boat captain, not our tour guide, who replied, "I'm not sure. Let's go see." He spun the boat around and followed the bird all the way back to its nest to identify it as an osprey. The purpose of the boat ride was to see seals, but the best part of the trip was when we deviated from the prescribed route and saw something that was not in the itinerary.

The most memorable experiences are not orchestrated (even though
I try to orchestrate such experiences as a professional naturalist).

Staged programming is not conducive to creating unique experiences. An aerial tour through the Grand Canyon has less chance of producing something memorable than a solo hike to the bottom. Guided tours are too predictable and too crowded. Also they put most of the burden of success on the guide rather than on the individual. Maybe most significantly, they move at a prearranged pace not conducive to lingering. This is not to say that planning should not be involved; good planning in good places helps to set up opportunities for special moments. Then when the special moment shows itself, the original plan is packed away like a windbreaker once the sun comes out.

Back in chapter 8 I described an incident involving Steve Van Matre at Disney World. I have my own Disney World story. When Clare was eleven, my daughter, my wife, my mom, and I spent six days there. I like Disney World, but it may be the most orchestrated place on the planet. One afternoon I needed a small break from the crowds and the subtle manipulation, so I retreated to an unoccupied sidewalk off the main thoroughfare of Frontierland. As I slowly walked along the pathway, a four-foot-long black snake slithered down the trail toward me. I realized I'd been in Disney World too long when my first thought was, "How'd they get that snake to do that?" I don't know anything about Floridian reptiles, but this lithe creature did not strike me as threatening. Immediately a Disney trash collector, one of the dozens of kids who wander the theme parks and pick up litter almost before it touches the ground, appeared directly behind the snake and said, "It's harmless, sir. It's called a black racer. It is fast, but gentle. You can back up if you want to, but if you stay where you are, it will come toward you until it's about five feet away, then it will turn to your right and climb over the short wall and disappear into the shrubbery. This is its home, and we are only visitors." The snake did exactly as the guy said it would (this was Disney World, after all), and before I could react, the kid was gone as quickly as the snake. I guess he had candy wrappers and discarded sales receipts to pick up. I wanted to ask the young man whether he'd been trained to deal with guest/snake encounters or was just innately aware. If the former, kudos to Disney. If the latter, the guy's talents were being wasted on litter detail.

Most memorable experiences are away from other people.

The only time I ever backpacked Yosemite, my hiking partner and I arrived by bus, meaning we also had to leave by bus. After seven days in the backcountry we dropped down into Yosemite Valley during Labor Day weekend. Our plan had been to spend two additional days in the valley checking out Half Dome and El Capitan before catching a bus back to San Francisco. We were still on the trail leading down from Clouds Rest, hadn't even reached the valley floor yet, when we were engulfed by tourists. On the trail, there were two lines of people moving in opposite directions, one walking up the trail to some unknown destination and another heading back down to the valley. I'd been to rock concerts less congested. My partner turned to me and declared that we needed to catch the first bus out of the park. Under normal circumstances, the crowds would have been bothersome—but not enough to chase us away.

However, after a week of wilderness backcountry where we'd encountered people in groups of two to four, the thought of sharing nature with ten thousand other tourists was unbearable. While in the backcountry, I'd decided Yosemite was the most spectacular natural area I'd ever seen. Neither my companion nor I wanted wall-to-wall people to be our last memory of the place. The absence of strangers is not an absolute when it comes to special moments in nature.[2] Still, there must be a positive correlation between memorable experiences and solitude.

A person has to be open to the magic.

Earlier I wrote that I do not understand Emerson. That is not entirely true. I understand him about 10 percent of the time and in small doses. Had none of his writings made sense to me, I would have given up a long time ago. Only because I comprehend tidbits do I keep coming back. One particular line from Emerson that does make sense is, "Nature always wears the colors of the spirit."[3] When I am outdoors, I fluctuate between thinking nature wants to tell me something very important and her not caring whether she tells me anything at all. Regardless of which of the two perspectives has greater veracity, it makes sense to interact with nature as if she is in communication. If Emerson's "colors of the spirit" is correct, then one prerequisite for seeing magic in nature is believing the magic exists.

Addendum

Earlier in this essay I wrote that I've experienced magical moments in the marsh near my home. I did not, however, offer a specific example. I do so now, as it points out the importance of frequent outings and an open mind.

Clare asked to borrow the binoculars. We'd already seen four other pairs of Canada geese and their newly hatched young on our after-dinner bicycle ride on the trails through the La Crosse River Marsh, but the family of geese before us now was different. All of the other groupings had one parent in the lead, the other in the rear, and two or three goslings swimming hard to maintain their secure positions in between. This new family of honkers was not so organized; they seemed to have goslings everywhere—behind the parents, in front of parents, alongside the parents—just about everywhere there could be a baby goose, there was a baby goose. I was content to watch the yellow mass of fluid fuzz encircle the surprisingly calm adults, but my nine-year-old daughter wanted the binoculars to count the exact number of young birds.

"Seventeen, Dad," she exclaimed. "There are seventeen babies. That must be a record."

"It's the most I've ever seen," I said.

"Me, too," she replied. "Do you think the mother laid seventeen eggs and they all hatched? Maybe all geese lay seventeen eggs, but foxes and raccoons eat them. Do you think that's it?"

"I don't know."

"Maybe some of the babies are orphans, their parents got shot and these parents adopted them. Do you think that's it?"

"No, it's not hunting season. Maybe another animal killed the adults, and some of the babies are orphans, but I guess all of the babies could have come from one nest."

"Well, I hope that the parents can take care of all those babies," Clare said. "At least they don't have to get milk from their mom like mammals. What do baby geese eat?"

Again I had to admit that I didn't know. We laid our bikes down in the reed canary grass and sat at water's edge. "Dad," Clare said, "the babies have lots of energy. They never stop moving."

She was right. The young geese moved with the energy of bees. The image that came to mind was the little plastic men on the electric football game I had as a kid—lots of jostling and vibrating and shifting of positions, but not much forward progress. Still, the family kept clustered together and, as a single tight unit, gradually worked its way across a small patch of open water.

Clare peppered me with more questions, most of which I could not answer. "How many babies do geese usually have?" "How long do the babies stay with the parents?" "How long does it take for the babies to learn to fly?" "Do you think just two parents can teach those babies all the stuff they need to know?" "When you see a bunch of geese flying together, do you think that's just one family?"

I, of course, was in dad heaven. My daughter's fascination with nature was transforming an otherwise uneventful Thursday into the highlight of my week. As with previous trips to the marsh, we visited not knowing what we might find, but on this particular evening we were being rewarded in spades. When the gaggle of geese disappeared into the young cattails along the opposite bank, Clare and I got back on our bikes and rode home.[4]

Part III

Continuums

17

The Preservationist and the Conservationist

The traditional way to define a relationship with the natural world is to assess whether a person is primarily a conservationist or a preservationist. This somewhat dated delineation has its limits, but it remains a good starting point upon which to build an environmental philosophy.

HETCH HETCHY IS A DEEP VALLEY IN THE SIERRA NEVADA MOUNTAINS.[1] Hikers in the late nineteenth century described it in superlative terms. John Muir himself wrote of it:

> It is estimated that about 7000 persons have seen Yosemite. If this multitude were to be gathered again, and set down in Hetch Hetchy perhaps less than one percent of the whole number would doubt their being in Yosemite. They would see rocks and waterfalls, meadows and groves, of Yosemite size and kind, and grouped in Yosemite style.[2]

Had Muir guided those seven thousand souls into Hetch Hetchy, they would have been among the last people on earth to gaze upon the valley in an undisturbed state. They would have been among the last people on earth to gaze upon the valley at all. In 1923, construction of the O'Shaughnessy Dam was completed, and Hetch Hetchy Valley disappeared 'neath the lapping tamed waters of Hetch Hetchy Reservoir.[3]

The significance of this saga is not so much the building of a dam as the events leading up to it. The Great San Francisco Earthquake occurred in 1906. The fires caused by the earthquake highlighted the fact that San Francisco did not have enough fresh water for its growing population. Soon after the quake, city leaders, always ready to take action *after* a crisis, proposed a dam and a 167-mile system of tunnels and aqueducts to bring pure water from Hetch Hetchy's Tuolumne River to the San Francisco Bay Area.

A sticking point to this public works project was that Hetch Hetchy resided within the boundaries of Yosemite National Park. In the early 1900s, the idea of a "nation's park"[4] was still a new concept. The National Park Service, the agency that would eventually oversee America's most spectacular landscapes, hadn't even been established yet.[5] General guidelines for what constituted an appropriate level of protection were still being worked out, but consensus was that national parks should remain more pristine than other public lands. The suggestion of a dam within Yosemite National Park was controversial.

Even with its national park designation, Hetch Hetchy might have been just another unnoticed assault on nature if not for two important factors. First were the personalities involved. Gifford Pinchot and John Muir, two of the foremost environmentalists of the day, entered the debate and took opposite sides. Pinchot, who had served as chief of the US Forest Service under Teddy Roosevelt, saw the damming of the Tuolumne as a perfect example of what good resource management ought to be—that is, the protection of a natural resource until its use is vital to the well-being of humankind. Pinchot was known for taking the quintessential utilitarian phrase "The greatest good for the greatest number" and adding to it "for the longest time."

Conversely "John of the Mountains" had lived in the Yosemite region and had been the driving force behind making Yosemite a national park in the first place. Even today Muir is considered by many American environmentalists to be the greatest preservationist of all time. He objected to the dam and publicly declared if national park designation did not protect a natural area from damming, then national park status had no meaning at all.

Secondly, and perhaps more significantly, Hetch Hetchy became a concrete (pun intended) symbol of the difference between conservation and preservation. Conservation is the wise and careful use of natural resources for the benefit of humankind. Natural areas should be carefully managed because they contain the basic raw materials for a thriving society. Preservation, on the other hand, is a viewpoint that once a determination has been made to preserve a piece of nature, it needs to be protected from further development. Preservationists often, but not always, are biocentric, meaning they believe nature itself has rights. From this perspective, nature should be protected not only because natural resources serve human needs, but also because nature has an intrinsic right to prosper.

I told the Hetch Hetchy story to a group of university students majoring in outdoor recreation. Most of them sided with Muir rather than Pinchot. It is the preservationist point of view, I suppose, that gives the tale its weight. Like a Shakespearian tragedy, there is not much to the story unless it ends badly. When I asked the students why they opposed the dam, the consensus was that a thing of beauty had been lost forever. This rationale provided the window I was looking for.

"So it's not," I said, "for ecological reasons. It is not because creatures great and small were forced out of their homes and a large patch of native vegetation was destroyed. You think the O'Shaughnessy Dam is wrong because you mourn the loss of beauty. Do I understand your reasons correctly? I want to be sure because it makes an important point."

Some of the students expanded their answer to include the destruction of habitat, but most still felt that their strongest sentiment was a visceral reaction to the flooding of a beautiful natural feature.

"Those of you who regret the loss of beauty," I said, "are reacting as preservationists, but your reason is based upon a human value, not a belief

in the intrinsic rights of nature. Sometimes we think the difference between conservation and preservation is that one cares about the needs
of people and the other cares about the needs of plants and animals. This
distinction will always be part of the conservationist–preservationist debate, but the bigger disagreement here is over two different *human* needs.
One is water, and the other is beauty.

"Think, for a moment, about all of the things we get from nature. We
get drinking water. We also get timber, minerals, food from the sea, and
land for grazing and agriculture. These are things we can see, measure,
and more or less hold in our hands. However, there are also benefits that
we can't hold. Solitude, challenge, peace of mind, a sense of place, and, as
you point out, beauty.[6] In the case of Hetch Hetchy, the dispute seems to
be between a tangible need and an abstraction.

"You identified natural beauty as a resource worth protecting. The
transcendentalist Ralph Waldo Emerson would have agreed with you. In
his essay *Nature*, he dedicated an entire section to the subject of beauty,
and when he made a comparison between intangible values and physical
resources such as timber and minerals, he wrote, 'A nobler want of man
is served by nature, namely, the love of Beauty.'"[7]

All of the students in my course had read *A Sand County Almanac*, so
I asked them to recall the essay "Thinking Like a Mountain." It is the story
of Leopold shooting a wolf in compliance with a Forest Service policy of
eradicating top predators. Leopold realizes the error of his actions when
he stands over the wounded animal and watches "a fierce green fire dying in her eyes."[8] I told the students that the young Leopold considered
himself a conservationist, not a preservationist. He trained as a forester
and then took a job with a conservation-oriented government agency.
Even so, working for the Forest Service was not always a good fit for the
man. Leopold held too many preservationist values to abide by all of
the agency's conservationist guidelines.[9] He left his field assignment
in the American Southwest and relocated to the Forest Service's research
facility in Wisconsin. Eventually he left the agency altogether, took a job
at a major university, and wrote *A Sand County Almanac*. Some have said

that Leopold's land ethic was his attempt to find the middle ground between extreme preservation and extreme conservation.[10] It is not a crazy
interpretation.

Nature–Human Philosophical Continuum No. 1

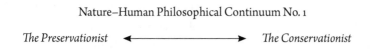

The Preservationist ←——————————→ *The Conservationist*

"Sometimes environmentalists are accused of being elitists," I said.
"They are seen as white guys living in upscale neighborhoods with expensive hybrid cars in the driveway. The criticism is valid, but I'd be a little
more specific. In my opinion, it is not all environmentalists who are elitists, but specifically those who identify as preservationists. These tend to
be the people with expensive homes and nice cars. They don't have oil re-
fineries or leaky landfills in their backyards. As a result, they have the luxury of focusing on matters other than personal health and safety. I consider myself one of these elitists."

"I've seen your car," chimed in one of the students. "It's not that nice."

"Yeah, but it has a roof rack for my kayak," I replied. "And that roof
rack symbolizes my brand of environmentalism. I connect to the natural world on a personal level through my recreation. I treasure wild places
as a place to play—and not only do I think everyone should care about
nature as much as I do, but I sometimes even want them to care about nature for the same reasons. That, I think, makes me an elitist. If you align
with John Muir and the preservationists, if you think natural beauty is
worth making sacrifices for, then you need to recognize and deal with
your own sense of self-righteous superiority. Don't sacrifice your principles, but don't lose your humility either. I doubt it would have made any
difference, but do you think any of us, even now, could make a convincing argument for sparing Hetch Hetchy simply because it was beautiful?
Can we or should we put a price on beauty?"

Because I taught in Wisconsin, most serious discussions about outdoor recreation eventually came around to hunting.[11] The students in the

class wanted to know whether hunters were conservationists by default because they extract a tangible resource from a pristine place. It turned out to be a good question. At the same time the hunters in the class sided more with Pinchot than the class as a whole, those same students were quick to point out they engaged in their favorite outdoor pursuit for all of the same intangible reasons nonhunters went to nature. They went for natural beauty, self-sufficiency, independence, challenge, and serenity. They even hunted for moral growth, if anyone would acknowledge that the decision to fire or not fire a weapon is a lesson in ethical behavior.[12] I have never had a vocal hunter in one of my classes who did not have a thoughtful response as to why he or she hunted.

When the issue of hunting was tossed back at me, I had a story for that, too.

🌿 🌿 🌿

Noted local birdwatcher Fred Lesher called me on the telephone. We knew each other well enough to greet one another at Earth Day celebrations and other environmental events, but the phone call might have been the first time we'd spoken one-on-one. Fred wanted to know, and these were the words he used, whether I'd be interested in "walking into the lion's den."

"The Conservation Congress," I replied.

"Yeah," he said. "If you are willing to go, you don't have to say anything. I'm just looking for bodies."

I agreed to go.

The Conservation Congress is the public arm of Wisconsin's resource management strategy. Meetings are held periodically across the state. Individuals voice their opinions, nonbinding votes are taken on current issues, and the results of those votes are passed on to the Department of Natural Resources (DNR). In theory, any resident of the state may attend the meetings. In practice, avid hunters dominate the room, and over the years nonhunters have gradually found reasons not to show up. A third of the attendees wear camouflage or blaze orange. They look like they came straight out of the woods to attend the meeting, when more than likely they just happened to have had enough time to go home after work to change into their hunting clothes.

Fred's interest in the upcoming meeting was because the big issue that year was whether to allow the hunting of mourning doves and sand-hill cranes. For years, the debate had been a back burner issue within the DNR, but recently several state legislators had been pushing for resolution. One congressman even brought mourning dove sandwiches to the Capitol and distributed them in the Rotunda. Fred knew the pro-hunting contingent would outnumber birdwatchers twenty-to-one, but he wanted the vote to show at least token dissent.

The meeting was held in a high school gym. It was well attended, about four hundred people scattered across bleachers on either side of the basketball court. Of the people who stepped to the microphone, Fred was the only one to speak on behalf of the birds. He was passionate and articulate. Even some of the hunters offered weak applause after his plea. Two separate hand votes were taken, one to support dove hunting, the other cranes. Only a couple dozen hands, mostly Lesher plants, went up in opposition to either recommendation.

Immediately after the count, a man sitting on my bleacher row, but fifteen feet away, walked over and sat down next to me. "I didn't expect anybody to vote against it," he said. "If you don't mind me asking, why did you?"

I explained it came down to killing something just for the sport of killing it. "I want another reason for shooting," I said. "Meat, overpopulation of a particular species, pest control, pelts. Something. Wisconsin hunters already have plenty of stuff to shoot. We aren't overrun by either doves or cranes, so why hunt them? I know you can get a few morsels of meat off a mourning dove, so I don't object to hunting them quite as strongly as the cranes, but what are you gonna do with a crane? Are you going to leave the carcass lying there for the coyotes?[13] I feel the same way about crows and woodchucks. Usually they aren't hurting anything and hardly anyone eats them—so I don't know why they should be shot."

"You don't hunt, do you?" asked the man.

"No. I fish, but I don't hunt."

"I didn't think so. I deer hunt and I duck hunt. Sometimes a little grouse and woodcock. I eat everything I kill, but it's not why I hunt. Nobody I know hunts because they need the meat. You probably don't fish to bring home fish either. We hunt to hunt. I probably won't hunt doves or cranes myself, but if a guy wants to hunt 'em when it's not deer season, it's all the same to me. I read up on this stuff before coming to the meeting, and everything I read says if we do the hunts right, it won't hurt numbers at all."

"So you are saying if you can shoot something without reducing its overall population, it's okay to do it?"

"Yeah, I guess I am," the man replied. "It's a renewable resource. It makes more sense than saying it's okay to hunt something only if I can come up with an excuse for shooting it. There is no such thing as catch-and-release hunting."

Even though we were only talking, I felt like I'd just lost an argument. From a strong preservationist perspective, I could have justified an across-the-board anti-hunting position. Had I gone in with an equally strong conservationist perspective, I'm sure I could have made a convincing pro-hunting defense. Dangling somewhere in the middle as I was, I could not explain, at least not convincingly, why I thought it was acceptable to shoot some species and not others. I hadn't figured out which preservationist value made me think that killing doves and cranes was unacceptable.

The man stood up, concluding our conversation. "Thanks," he said. "You've given me something to think about." I sensed it was said mostly as a courtesy.

18

The Wanderer and the Adventurer

In Chinese landscape paintings, there sometimes is evidence of a human presence. It might be a structure such as a small pedestrian bridge or a gazebo. It might be an actual person, someone boating on a river or walking along a trail. Because the natural elements in the paintings are on a grand scale, usually depicting an entire mountain or an entire river valley, the human features are hard to find and intentionally unassuming. In all instances, as far as I have observed, the human element reflects a gentle interaction with the natural world. If there is anyone on the river, the person is poling a boat on flat water, not battling whitewater in a tiny canoe. If there is someone on the mountain, the person is walking alone on a winding trail, not scaling a sheer cliff. If there is a person at the gazebo, the individual is drinking tea alone or playing Chinese chess with a friend. When I see a Chinese landscape ink drawing, I always look for the human presence. If I find someone in the art, I mentally put myself in that person's place.

DURING THE SUMMER OF 2019, THE UPPER MISSISSIPPI RIVER REMAINED at flood stage late into the summer. High water in April and May is normal. High water in July is not. I wanted to paddle, but not in the rapidly flowing main channel, so I put in at a quiet piece of backwater called Black Deer. Black Deer is a narrow sheltered watercourse north of La Crosse, really not much more than a wide ditch running parallel to the Mississippi River proper. By midsummer it usually is too weedy for any watercraft. That year, however, because of the high water, there remained an open lane more than wide enough for a canoe.

I paddled upstream all the way to Black Deer's source, which turned out to be a long culvert. The culvert's diameter was about three feet, its length maybe sixty feet. I looked through the tube and saw blue sky at the far end. I paddled the bow of my canoe into the mouth of the culvert and discovered a clearance about the width of my hand. Had the water level been any lower, the bottom of the culvert would have been higher than the surface of the river, and the canoe would not have slipped into the opening. Had the water level been any higher, river water would have taken up most of the space in the culvert and left no room for my boat. As it was, I was able to lie flat in the bottom of my canoe and push myself and my boat hand over hand through the tunnel. Highly adventurous people might not see this as a challenge at all, but they'd be wrong. Challenge is not an objective measure. It is each person facing his or her own fears and testing personal boundaries. Entering a confined space no wider or higher than my canoe unnerved me. Still, I could not resist.

I moved along briskly until I reached the far end. There, free-floating tree branches and broken cattails jammed the exit, and my boat got stuck. My claustrophobia, which had been under control until then, kicked in. Fortunately I was able to wriggle forward in my canoe just enough to get my hands on the outer edge of the culvert. This gave me the leverage I needed to force the bow of my canoe through the debris. I cut my fingers on the sharp lip of the corrugated metal, but made it out. The far side opened up into a broad marsh. I explored the area for an hour, then returned to Black Deer by going back through the culvert. The return trip went with the current, and I'd already dislodged all of the obstructions, so I easily floated through.

When I told a few friends about my little adventure, all of them replied in different ways that I had been stupid to do what I had done. They all wanted to know what would have happened had I really gotten stuck. The most adamant was a friend from New Mexico. She told me every year someone drowns in New Mexico's irrigation ditches, and often the tragedy happens because someone gets trapped in a culvert. Albuquerque even has a Ditch and Water Safety Task Force with the message "Ditches Are Deadly—Stay Away! Find Safe Places to Swim and Play."

My friends' warnings did get me to think about my reasons for squeezing into the confined space. If, however, their main objective was to make me more cautious, it backfired. Before they chewed me out, I wondered why I'd bitten on the culvert gauntlet in the first place. After their admonitions, the question evolved into a desire to understand why I didn't succumb to comparable challenges more often.

Two Sides of the Same Coin

Peacefulness and challenge are not contradictions so much as complementary opposites. A discussion of one opens a door to the other. A sense of peace, such as is achieved by canoeing a gentle stretch of river, deliberately puts a person deeply into a comfort zone. Challenge, such as canoeing big water slightly beyond a person's paddling skills, intentionally takes that person outside of any comfort zone. The two activities differ from each other, but they both help people to temporarily put daily routines aside. One activity floats a person into a wonderful sense of serenity, and the other demands so much of a person's attention that he or she does not have time to think about other petty concerns.

When I actively seek challenge, I think of myself as an *adventurer*. When I go to nature in hopes of finding peace, I usually wander. I am a *wanderer*. These two descriptors work as well as any to name the interdependent duality involved here.

Nature–Human Philosophical Continuum No. 2

The Wanderer ⟵————————⟶ *The Adventurer*

On the far right of this continuum, adventurers bring themselves to the brink of risking their lives. On the far left, wanderers seek the ultimate quietude with a camera or a sketch pad or a book of poetry. Adventurers make their hearts race; wanderers intentionally slow their hearts down. Adventurers view an encounter with nature as a test; wanderers go to nature to avoid being tested. The fact that nature can appeal to us in two such different ways, and no one thinks it odd, says a lot about the wonder of the nature–human relationship.

Age

It may be an overgeneralization to even suggest this, but people's motivations for going to nature tend to change over time. In terms of adventure and wandering, many young people go to nature for excitement, old-timers not so much. With age, the need for adventure wanes. People mature and start to realize they are not immortal. They regress physically, and their bodies remind them they have limits. They assume more and more obligations in daily life, so activities that can be described as carefree, as opposed to careless, become increasingly attractive. Over time, individuals gradually move toward the wanderer side of the continuum, so much so that those who remain hardcore adventurers into late middle age sometimes are accused of not growing up at all.[1]

Years ago I taught an activity-oriented outdoor recreation course. We caved, canoed, and did a variety of other outdoor activities every Monday afternoon. Almost all of the students were in their early twenties. At the end of one of the semesters, during the students' final evaluation of the course, I told the students my travel budget for field trips was being cut. I then asked them to identify one activity I must absolutely keep in the course and one that probably could go. One student pretty much summed up the opinion of the class as a whole when she said, "I don't think I can pick a favorite, but I'd dump birdwatching. Maybe I'll look at birds when I am fifty. Right now it is boring."

The words were no sooner out of the woman's mouth when she realized I was about fifty years old at the time and a big fan of birdwatching. She tried to backtrack her comments to the amusement of the other students, and I jokingly assured her that I appreciated her honesty and would lower her grade for the course by no more than a full letter. These particular young adults were not interested in non-adventurous encounters with nature. They saw peaceful wandering as something for people much older than themselves.

The most significant moment of the Black Deer canoe adventure was not getting stuck in the culvert. It was not getting unstuck. It was not seeing what was on the other side. It was the moment I realized that the bow of the canoe fit into the small entrance of the culvert and I knew I was going in. In an instant, I'd gone from an old wanderer to someone who still possessed a sense of adventure.

Less So the Activity
Than the Mindset

Even though there is a tendency to characterize some forms of recreation as innately adventurous and others as innately peaceful, most outdoor pursuits do not fit into neat wanderer–adventurer categories. Canoeing, for example, runs the full gamut. There is Class IV and Class V water that is potentially dangerous even to skilled paddlers, and there is water so flat and peaceful that it does not receive a level-of-difficulty rating at all. There also is plenty of paddleable water somewhere in between.

No activity, not even one generally associated with either end of the wanderer–adventurer spectrum, is ever all wander or all adventure. Like the interlocking "tadpoles" of the classic symbol for the yin and the yang (the T'ai-chi-t'u), each side of the complementary opposites has a seed of the other in it. It is how a quiet day of paddling on Black Deer becomes an adventure. It is how a morning of whitewater paddling concludes with beached kayaks and a relaxing lunch on the riverbank. In terms of outdoor activities, the balance between challenge and peace always comes down to the desired outcomes of the person undertaking the pursuit.

Sometimes I think the wanderer–adventurer continuum is more a circle than a straight line. By this I mean that the elements at the far ends of the continuum begin to look like each other. This is most evident in super-serious outdoorsmen and women who take their activities to unusual extremes. An example is the fanatical birdwatcher who travels halfway around the world to tromp through miles of jungle for a glimpse of a rare hornbill or parrot. A pastime that may have started out as serene morphs into challenging adventure. Or maybe it was the other way around. Maybe the world traveler was an adventurer all along and could not keep challenge out of a pursuit that is normally peaceful and serene.

This notion of coming full circle on the wanderer–adventurer continuum is supported by Mihaly Csikszentmihalyi's theory of flow.[2] According to Csikszentmihalyi, highly skilled recreationists who undertake difficult tasks go into a hyper-focused autopilot and literally become part of the experience. Even though they take on vertical granite faces or Class IV whitewater, they describe the experience as calm immersion. It is as if they stepped off the adventurer end of the continuum and discovered a deep sense of peace. When highly skilled climbers or paddlers achieve flow, they are dead serious when they say they've become one with the rock or one with the water. They've transcended challenge, and it is hard for the rest of us not to be envious.

So What?

On the wanderer–adventurer continuum, I am unable to pinpoint my exact location. Instead, I put myself in a fairly wide band left of center. I no longer intentionally seek big challenges, but I still have a hard time resisting minor ones when my wanderings evolve into something more bold.

The Wanderer ←———————→ *The Adventurer*

In trying to find my place on the continuum, I came to the following conclusions about my relationship with the natural world:

1. Even as a young man, I most enjoyed activities
that were not risky or adventurous.

I rock climbed and whitewater paddled when I was young, but even then I preferred fishing and watching wildlife. Often when my friends were scaling rock faces, I went fishing. They would drive for hours to find a good place to climb, and I would drive an equal distance to find a new place to fish. When I went rock climbing with those friends, I did it more for the companionship than for the thrill of the challenge. When I was a young adult, I was more adventurous than I am now, but not as adventurous as many of my friends.

2. For over thirty years I took people into nature, and I never
learned to relax when I taught high-risk activities.

Even though I knew climbing and whitewater paddling and caving were safe when taught properly, I was constantly preoccupied with the safety of my students. Adventurous pursuits were entertaining when done on my own time, but I was never totally at ease when I taught them to others. Conversely, when I taught people to notice the beauty of nature through hikes and birdwatching and exploring tide pools, I found I could teach students and enjoy myself at the same time. Work-related activities do not necessarily transfer to a person's leisure pursuits, but the outdoor recreation I most enjoyed teaching to others became the recreation I most enjoyed on my own.

3. I feel closest to nature when I am quietly
wandering the natural world alone.

I intellectually understand a person may find a oneness with nature when challenging himself or herself to the limit, but I have never felt that way myself. I most feel a connection with nature when I am in my canoe on a quiet backwater with a fishing pole in my hand. For me, the key component to a oneness with nature is solitude. High-risk activities, if done safely, are not done alone.

4. Maybe I am just lazy when it comes to my leisure.

The most ardent adventurers work very hard at their recreational pursuits. Lifelong participation in high-risk activities requires a continuous honing of skills. A fair amount of negative press has been given to wealthy novices who spend thousands of dollars to hire the expertise needed to confront Mount Everest, but the majority of the climbers on world-class mountains are highly skilled mountaineers who have climbed all their lives and have kept in exceptional physical shape. They train hard for months prior to their big ascents. I admire these people's dedication to their avocation. I also realize I don't want to work that hard in my own leisure. Even though I take my outdoor recreation seriously, I want it to be carefree and easy.

5. When it is all said and done, I want to be the
person in a Chinese landscape painting.

19

The Homecomer and the Sojourner

Nature is holistic, but our connection to nature may come to us in seg-ments. As Ralph Waldo Emerson put it, "We see the world piece by piece," and then must cobble those pieces together if we hope to witness nature's soul.[1] I agree with Emerson's assessment, but wonder if it makes a differ-ence whether our collection of individually packaged special moments in nature happen mostly at home or mostly away from home.

THERE IS AN ENVIRONMENTAL EDUCATION ACTIVITY FOR ELEMENTARY school–age children called a micro-hike.[2] Students are paired up, and each small team is given five feet of kite string and a half dozen flagged tooth-picks. The assignment is to identify points of interest on a "hike" only as long as the string. The objective is to focus on small aspects of nature that usually go unnoticed. For years I carried a manila envelope with string and toothpicks in my naturalist bag of tricks, but can count on one hand the number of times I actually pulled it out to use with kids.

I know why I conducted micro-hikes so infrequently. As much as I wanted students to hone their observation skills, the exercise felt too de-tailed for most situations. The purist in me wants to believe none of us can ever be too detailed when it comes to observing nature, but that is not true. When I worked with children, it was mostly city and suburban kids who'd spent very little time in any kind of natural setting. Five feet of ground seemed something to investigate only after the big, more spectacular stuff had been checked out, and I was rarely with the kids long enough for that to happen. There were woods to hike, marshes to explore, and hillsides to scramble up. Why would children, or most adults for that matter, want to look at a dead bug or a half-decomposed leaf when there were hundred-foot redwood trees or fuzzy baby geese to see? Any naturalist who has been showing kids an interesting pattern in the veins of a dogwood leaf when a doe and a fawn enter the clearing understands that spectacular nature trumps the details.

To me, the difference between a micro-hike and a conventional one-foot-in-front-of-the-other hike captures a difference between nature at home and nature away. On a micro-hike, we take the time to search out and appreciate the little things after we've experienced a place's more sensational attributes. On a conventional hike, especially on a trail we've never walked before, everything is so new we tend to engage at a macro level. For all I know, John Muir micro-hiked the heck out of Yosemite. I, however, spent only one week there on a meandering trek from Tuolumne Meadows to the valley floor. I never got beyond gawking at Cathedral Peak, Clouds Rest, and the black bears that came into camp most nights. Give me a year or two in Yosemite, and maybe the granite landscapes and charismatic megafauna would become commonplace enough for me to want to look at the meadow grass through a magnifying lens.

Microbiologists undoubtedly would disagree with me on this matter, and I readily admit to a bias in this regard. All I can say is that when the content of both my Intro to Botany course and my Intro to Zoology course were at the cellular rather than the ecosystem level, I dropped biology as my undergraduate major and switched to resource management. To this day, I am bothered that students in many introductory biology labs spend most of their time looking through a microscope.

Defining the Terms of This Continuum

Of the four continuums described in part III of this book, I had the hardest time, but also the most fun, naming this one. Both *homecomer* and *sojourner* are quirky terms and not obvious choices.

Nature–Human Philosophical Continuum No. 3

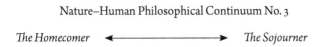

The Homecomer ←—————————→ *The Sojourner*

For the left side of the continuum, I chose the word *homecomer.* I wrote the first draft of this chapter without knowing what the representative term would be. Initially I was drawn to "settler" as a name, except that settler connotes a person who originally comes from one place, then makes a home somewhere else. I needed a word that described both new members to a particular community and anyone born to the place. I used the word "dweller" for a while, but really hoped it was only a placeholder. I was resigned to going with dweller when I ran across "homecomer" in Wes Jackson's *Becoming Native to This Place.* He defined a homecomer not as a prodigal son coming home after years of wanderlust, but as anyone who immerses himself or herself in a particular locale with plans to conduct "the long search and experiment to become native."[3] Jackson's definition was exactly what I was looking for.

On naming the other side of the spectrum, I toyed with the term "wayfarer," but eventually went with *sojourner.* Both terms refer to travelers, the former word emphasizing the mode of transportation and the latter the pace. A wayfarer is a person who travels by foot. A sojourner is a person on a long journey, but a journey with extended stopovers between periods on the move.

I had not finalized my decision between these two good options when I serendipitously decided to make one of my periodic attempts at understanding Emerson's *Essays.* Failing again at that endeavor, I put Emerson aside and pulled out my old copy of *Walden.* Although I would never call *Walden* light reading, Thoreau has become my fallback option when I am overwhelmed by Emerson. I usually open *Walden* at random and read whatever chapter catches my eye. This time I started at the beginning. In the opening passages, Thoreau explains that his two years alone at Walden Pond are over and he is back in Concord. He concludes the first paragraph of the book by saying that he is again "a *sojourner* in civilized life."[4] If Thoreau could describe his life away from Walden as that of a sojourner, the word worked for me in defining my life away from home.

Nature, Home and Away

This chapter is based upon what I consider a fairly solid, but unsubstantiated, assumption that our interactions with nature at home differ from those away from home. At home, we experience the subtle details as much as we do the obvious elements. We notice changes over time, something not possible with short-term stays. We observe both the commonplace and the rare, and we know which is which when we see them. Home also is where we leave our physical mark. We volunteer on conservation projects. We rip out exotic shrubs in our yard and replace them with native species. We dig up a corner of the lawn to make a garden that over the years goes from a bare piece of ground to an elaborate arrangement of raised beds and permanent trellises. We become an active member of the community, and that community includes its nonhuman elements.

Compared to home, places away from home are less personal, but they sometimes are more spectacular. The places we visit usually are not chosen at random. We intentionally seek out some of the most awe-inspiring settings on the planet, so the highlights there tend to be more jaw-dropping than anything we see in our neighborhoods. All of us need to be occasionally overwhelmed by the exceptional wonders of nature, but a dazzling sense of awe is not the same thing as intimacy.

Table 1 summarizes some of the distinctions between relating to nature from home and relating to her from places not home. The lists contrast the familiar with the unknown, the intimate with the grand, and the local perspective with a global one. Readers will find exceptions to the table's descriptors of home and away. I do. For example, every autumn twenty-five thousand migrating tundra swans stop to rest on the Mississippi Flyway only a few miles from my house. In this case, the spectacular does happen at home, just as intimacy sometimes occurs in faraway places. Readers probably can come up with an exception to just about every box in the home/not home table, but in general, the stated distinctions tend to point out common differences in our encounters with nature at home and away.

Table 1. Exploring Nature at Home and Everywhere Else

HOME	NOT HOME
Sense of place and community	A need to satisfy wanderlust
Intimate	Grandiose
The familiar	The unknown (the other)
Same place over time (seasonality)	Different places for a short time (snapshots)
Small wonders	The spectacular
Snail's pace (time not a factor)	On the move (time is a factor)
Alter the resource (often restore it)	Practice minimum impact
Let nature come to us	Actively seek out nature
Narrowly focused (bioregional)	A worldview
Representative books	Representative books
Walden	*A Thousand-Mile Walk to the Gulf*
Pilgrim at Tinker Creek	*The Voyage of the Beagle*
The Outermost House	*Canoeing with the Cree*

The question then becomes whether these different encounters define our relationship with nature in different ways. Henry David Thoreau rarely left New England, whereas John Muir had a hard time sitting still long enough to write about his travels. The two most well-known nature writers in American literature used opposite approaches to experience nature. Obviously both methods form the building blocks for a solid nature–human relationship. Still, I have to believe the resulting relationships differ from each other.

The Difference May Be a Frame of Mind

It takes more than settling down to make a homecomer, more than traveling to make a sojourner. It is a person's head and heart that determine the perspective. Some adults live in the house they grew up in, but still are not native to the land. They do not know the habits of the most common birds in their neighborhood, the right time of the year to plant cucumbers, or the history of the people indigenous to the region. They lack the important homecomer attribute of wanting to continuously learn more about their place.

Conversely there are travelers who flit through locations so quickly and superficially they cannot be described as sojourners. There may not be an ideal length of time for a stop during a sojourn, but it is measured in days and weeks, not hours. I have done my share of quick visits. While zipping through a tourist destination might be better than not going there at all, a lasting connection with a natural wonder (or an urban one, for that matter) seldom occurs when the total interaction is taking a few photographs with a cellphone and having lunch at the visitor center's cafeteria.

Homecomers explore as enthusiastically as sojourners, but do it in a confined area. Sojourners probe just as seriously as homecomers; they just do it on the move. Annie Dillard expressed the homecomer sentiment by writing, "I explore the neighborhood."[5] In contrast, John Muir nailed the sojourner perspective by writing, "The world's big and I want to have a good look at it before it gets dark."[6] And Tim Paterson tried to capture it all by saying, "Travel is a matter of perspective, not location."[7]

Still, Homecomers and Sojourners Tend to Interpret Experiences Differently

It is not uncommon for a sojourner to point out something to a local resident, who then responds, "Oh, wow. I'd never noticed that before." For example, I have been in La Crosse for over twenty years, and once or twice a

year a friend visits and shows me something that may not have gone unnoticed, but had been underappreciated. This happens because homecomers and sojourners bring with them different observation skills and
different wells of knowledge.

I often fish Pool 8 on the Mississippi River. Pool 8 is unique on the
Upper Mississippi because it is part of a case study. The Army Corps of
Engineers maintains the pool's summer water level lower than the adjacent pools. The purpose is to increase aquatic plant life, and the experiment has worked better than some recreationists like. I fish from my
kayak, so I can still go just about anywhere in the pool, but motorboaters, unless they want to constantly untangle eelgrass from their propellers, are restricted to a limited number of deeper channels.

As a homecomer on the Upper Mississippi River, I have personally
witnessed the changes to Pool 8 over time. How would a one-time visitor perceive the same place and the same situation? She would not have
the chronological information I possess. She would not know the vegetation was thicker in 2021 than in previous summers. She might not realize the Corps of Engineers lowers water levels on the pool every summer.
She might not even know the Corps is capable of adjusting the water levels. She would have no reason to know that Pool 8 was intentionally shallower than Pools 7 and 9.

Although a sojourner visiting the Upper Mississippi would not have
site-specific information readily at hand, she would have knowledge of
other rivers as a basis of comparison. What if, for example, she had recently spent several weeks along the Mekong River in Southeast Asia?
Her mind would race to the differences and similarities between two exceptional waterways half a world apart. She might notice the local people in Laos play on their river as enthusiastically as Midwesterners play
on theirs. She'd conclude that Thai three-plank boats with their extended
propellers handle shallow weedy water better than American speedboats,
but not quite as well as kayaks. She would wonder whether the channel
catfish pulled out of the Mississippi River were a close relative to the whis
kered fish she ate at a riverfront restaurant in Champasak. She'd observe

that goods on the Mekong are transported in small quantities by small boats, whereas freight traffic on the Mississippi moves cargo up and down the river in barges the size of small warehouses.

A patient homecomer might bring a sojourner up to speed on the uniqueness of Pool 8, and a sojourner could offer the homecomer a fresh perspective. My strongest impression of a homecomer and a sojourner together in the same locale is not that two people see the river differently (which they do). It is that they teach each other and fill in gaps. One perspective deals in the specifics of a single location; the other draws comparisons across locations.

None of This Is to Suggest Sojourners Don't Experience Intimacy

Jennifer Lilla, the naturalist at the Trempealeau National Wildlife Refuge, once offered an interesting insight about locale. On one of my visits with students, she mentioned that the job at the refuge was her third placement within the Department of the Interior. The first two had been the Everglades in Florida and the North Cascades in the state of Washington. Even though I myself had left the grandeur of California's redwoods for the less spectacular Upper Mississippi River Valley, I was stunned by Jenny's decision to relocate. "Then what are you doing here?" I blurted out.

Her reply was immediate and spot on. "I requested the transfer," she said. "Those other places were sometimes too much. Every morning I would marvel at the wonders just outside of the staff housing, but I also always felt like I was living in a national park, which I was. Here the nature is equally beautiful, but at a human scale. It is here I feel at home."

Although Jenny did not specifically use the word, she was talking about intimacy. I, like just about everyone else, am attracted to the great natural wonders of the world, but even among the great wonders, I most remember the small moments that could have just as well happened elsewhere. The spectacular brought me to the place, but it was the intimate moment within the spectacular that left a lasting mark.[8]

For example, my most memorable experience in Yosemite National Park was as intimate as it was unexpected. Camping one evening in the shadow of Cathedral Peak, Lisa, my hiking partner, and I spread out our Ensolite pads and sleeping bags side by side to watch the stars come out. The high mountain air turned chilly as soon as the sun set behind a ridge, so we slipped under our bags with only our heads sticking out. Suddenly, without warning, a great horned owl with extended talons appeared a few feet in front of our faces. Instinctively I shot up my arms and tossed my sleeping bag. Afterward I found out Lisa's reaction had been exactly the same. I doubt I'd averted my eyes from the owl for even a full second, but by the time I looked again, it was gone. For an instant, I feared for my eyes. Immediately afterward and from that point on, I relished the time I was so much an element of nature that an owl mistook me for prey.

My most memorable experience at the Grand Canyon is equally small and personal. When I think back to my trip there, I would describe my initial sighting from the South Rim of the canyon as a disappointment. The view was stunning, but too much like the postcards. If special moments have an element of surprise to them, then standing at the edge of the Grand Canyon did not qualify. The view was pretty much what I'd expected. In contrast, the hike to the bottom of the canyon down the South Kaibab Trail and then out of the canyon up the Bright Angel Trail was one of the most memorable backpacking loops I've ever taken. It was January, so the change in elevation went from cold weather to warm. I saw elk for the first time in my life. Until that hike, I didn't even know the Grand Canyon was actually two distinct geological features, the broad dry upper canyon that appears in all of the photographs and the less harsh, oasis-like inner canyon, so much narrower than the top half that it cannot be seen in most photos taken from the rim.

And what most sticks in my mind about my backpacking trip to the bottom of the Grand Canyon? It is that I did not pack enough food for the hike out. On most backpacking trips, I spend the last night only a few miles from the trailhead. This gives me one last night in the backcountry. The next morning I break camp quickly without bothering to eat, hike to my car, then treat myself by driving directly to the nearest restaurant for a late breakfast. On those trips, however, my trip is an exact loop, and I exit the wilderness right at my car. On the Grand Canyon trip, I exited the canyon at a different spot than where I started, and my car was still miles away. Also on most of my backcountry trips, I am coming out of mountains, meaning the last few miles are hiking downhill. Gravity is working with me, and each step, while sometimes hard on the knees, takes almost no effort. Exiting the Grand Canyon was a steady 10 percent uphill grade. Without breakfast, the ascent called for an energy reserve I did not have. After the initial half hour of hiking, simply walking became difficult, and I realized I was experiencing real hunger for maybe the first time in my life. When I finally made it to the top of the canyon, I was angry because the restaurant and all of the other touristy amenities were still a half mile away. I wanted there to be a gift shop with snacks the moment I came up over the rim. There was only a parking lot and a viewing platform. Under normal conditions, a vending machine at the trailhead would have disgusted me. That morning I would have paid ten dollars for a candy bar.

I do not wish to minimize the significance of anyone's encounters with spectacular nature. If someone was moved to tears at her first rim-top sighting of the Grand Canyon, it may show a connection with nature I don't possess. I will venture a guess, however, that the tearful moment did not come while standing side by side with a hundred other tourists all jostling to get a selfie of themselves with no one else in the frame. Whether intimacy or awe, strong emotions are more likely to occur when a person gets away from the crowds.

And There Is In-Between

I've kept the same copy of *Walden* for over forty years. The binding has gone brittle. Every time I open the book now, another dozen pages break off from the spine. A couple more readings and I will not have a book at all, just a tattered cover wrapped around sequentially ordered sheets of paper. Still, I read this battered copy of *Walden* for the same reason I read my original copy of *A Sand County Almanac*. It is for the comments written in the margins. As I peruse Thoreau or Leopold for the twentieth time, I revisit all of my past interpretations by scanning my comments and rereading the highlighted passages. In retrospect, I wish I'd dated my comments. I am intrigued by how much my reactions to certain sections change over time. There are passages that move me now, but had not in the past. That I would expect, as with age comes new insights. There are also, however, passages that must have been important to me forty years ago, but today fail to leave an impression. If not for the fact that I recognize the handwriting in the margins as my own, I would have guessed the comments had been made by someone else.

For example, next to the passage about Thoreau leaving Walden Pond and returning to Concord, I'd written, "Why only one extreme or the other? Can't I be somewhere in between?" The words are mine, but I don't remember ever writing them or even thinking them. Now I wonder where I was mentally when I made the notation.

And while I no longer identify with that particular note in the margin, I can still agree with it. As with all continuums, homecomer–sojourner is not an either/or, all-or-nothing proposition. There is the huge area on the continuum between the two extremes. What is the middle ground between homecomer and sojourner? When I asked, "Why only one extreme or the other?" I am guessing I was an underclassman in college. At the time, my strongest connections with nature came from childhood, and many of my special childhood moments were neither at home nor on a sojourn. If any single natural place was special to me during my early years, it was Door County's Peninsula State Park. The park's Weborg Point was where my family took a vacation every June. An excursion to the same place year after year was not like Thoreau's two-year stint at Walden, but neither was it a one-time road trip. It was, as I once noted in the margins of my worn copy of *Walden*, the somewhere in-between.

Now that I have moved back to Wisconsin after two decades of sojourning, I visit Weborg Point every year or so. I don't camp there anymore. Setting up a tent thirty feet from someone else's motor home no longer appeals to me.[9] Still, I like to spend an afternoon there, although the time is more about reminiscing than adding new experiences. As a kid, it was at Weborg Point where dozens of nature-related firsts occurred. It is where I used an artificial fishing lure for the first time in my life, where I watched raccoons raid the garbage cans every night (but sensed there was something wrong with the practice), and where I begged my dad not to drive over the hundreds of frogs that hopped onto the entrance road on rainy nights.[10]

The homecomer–sojourner continuum has an underlying aspect to it that seems different from the other continuums described in this book. In comparison to the homecomer–sojourner continuum, the others feel like ends in themselves. Finding our place on the other continuums helps us to see who we are in relation to the natural world, but doesn't necessarily ask us to use the realization for any particular action. For example, once I realized I was more a preservationist than a conservationist, I did not feel the need to explore what it meant to be a preservationist. Just knowing my perspective helped me to understand that my opinions on certain environmental issues came from a preservationist point of view. In contrast, the homecomer–sojourner continuum is more a starting point than a clarification of an environmental perspective. After I determine who I am in terms of homecoming and sojourning, I feel the need to go out and enhance my connection with nature accordingly. More than the other continuums, the homecomer–sojourner continuum is a reminder to spend even more time outside.

20

The Romantic and the Scientist

In this chapter I discuss the last of four continuums. It is different from the other three in one important way. It is the only one to have undergone a significant societal shift in the last half century. If individuals of baby boomer age have moved from their position on the preservationist–conservationist, wanderer–adventurer, or homecomer–sojourner continuums, it is a result of personal changes, not because society has nudged them off their marks. With the romantic–scientist continuum, however, society itself moved, and a person might have been carried along by the cultural transformation.

DURING THE QUESTION AND ANSWER PORTION OF A CONFERENCE PRE-sentation, environmental theologian Elizabeth Dodson Gray was asked to describe one example of ecofeminism in action.[1] A woman in the audience said she appreciated the parallels between humanity's domination of nature and society's subjugation of women, but was having a hard time translating the comparison into anything tangible. Without hesitation, Dodson Gray answered, "Raptor rehabilitation programs." She went on to explain that the nurturing and the intense nature–human relationships associated with caring for and retraining injured eagles, hawks, and owls exemplified ecofeminism.

Immediately a voice in the back of the room exclaimed, "I hate raptor rehabilitation programs." Dodson Gray's talk had been standing room only, and a guy who'd been leaning against the back wall stepped forward. He immediately stated that he loved raptors, his life was dedicated to the protection of bald eagles, but he cared more about the viability of the species than saving a few birds. He accused raptor rehabilitation programs of siphoning hard work and finite resources away from habitat restoration. He said rehabilitation programs created a false sense that something significant was being done when it wasn't and suggested the rehabilitation of individual raptors was more about making humans feel good about themselves than about doing anything that benefited wildlife or ecosystems. He acknowledged well-intentioned people were acting with their hearts, but felt the issue of endangered and threatened species was too important to be driven by sentimentality. Environmentalists who cared about raptors needed to rely upon scientific principles rather than heartstrings to strategically focus their efforts.

I was at the Dodson Gray presentation that day, and my first thought was, "I like raptor rehabilitation programs, but I don't see the flaw in the guy's argument." It took me a few days to figure it out. The flaw, if flaw is even the right word, was the man's limited focus. He was unwilling to consider any benefit other than habitat restoration. He thought people's personal relationships with nature were irrelevant. He saw releasing a single bird to the wild as a pointless symbolic gesture. He cared only about results and not a lick about process.

Where did the eagle man develop such an outlook? My sense is that the answer to this question is more about when than where. His steadfast logical and scientific way of looking at nature came from the second half of the twentieth century, which is the same source as most of my nature-related values and beliefs. The reason I had trouble identifying the weaknesses in the man's tirade was because I was so much like him.

In 1999, *Time* magazine's Person of the Century was Albert Einstein.[2] The magazine's editors wrote that the final hundred years of the second millennium would be remembered as the Century of Science, and no one represented the time better than the man who personified contemporary scientific thought.

If one period of time is identified as one thing, there is an implication that the period to follow will be something else. Late in the twentieth century, environmentalists, theologians, futurists, even scientists predicted that this new thing, this new way of thinking, would be a gradual shift away from absolute faith in science. In its place would be an awareness that (1) science alone cannot answer all questions and (2) the scientific method and more intuitive ways of thinking are not mutually exclusive. Some called this new perspective spiritual ecology, a term that would have been an oxymoron a few decades earlier. Others called it the ecological age. Regardless of the terminology, it is not a rejection of biology, physics, chemistry, and the more quantitative aspects of the social sciences. It is an integration of science with other sources of knowledge. These other sources include philosophy, theology, mythology, anthropology (i.e., indigenous people's understanding of humanity's place in the world), literature, and art. It is not one discipline displacing another, but a conscious effort to do away with intellectual silos and to "honor both art and science."[3] Catholic priest Thomas Berry saw it as a return to the spiritual traditions of the past, but with a big difference—that difference being that the new spirituality is built upon an informed knowledge base significantly enhanced by an era of science and technology.[4] Although I shouldn't even have to say it, the ecological age is not permission to disregard science just because its conclusions are distasteful. Environmental educator David Orr wrote of the subject, "Fundamentalists have mistaken the relation between passion, emotion, and good science. These are not antithetical, but complexly interdependent."[5]

Nature–Human Philosophical Continuum No. 4

The Romantic ◄─────────── ► *The Scientist*

For me (and I assume many others of my generation), the transition from extreme faith in science to a more balanced approach has been welcome, but not seamless. Whereas many recent insights on the environment have confirmed and strengthened my long-established science-based value system,[6] the ecological age has forced me to question some aspects of it. I sometimes feel pulled in two directions. At the same time that I celebrate a broad-based approach to environmentalism, part of me wants to stay on the scientific end of the spectrum. By that, I mean I enjoy the transition to the ecological age, but continue to rely upon scientific approaches (i.e., logic, analysis, direct use of the senses, and linear thinking) to solve my environmental quandaries. I tend not to trust intuition or spiritual faith—not my own and certainly not that of others. Neither am I particularly moved by theater and dance intended to raise environmental consciousness. I cling to the belief that when science cannot explain something, it is only because science has yet to figure it out.

My millennial daughter might be surprised by my struggles with multiple modes of thinking. First of all, her education has been multifaceted, so my steadfast adherence to the scientific method is foreign to her. Secondly, she has seen me inhale nature-based literature and environmental philosophy, so she would not understand why they are not an integral part of my thought processes. Finally, she knows I have a fascination with the magic of nature, and she has observed me enjoy moments in the natural world that cannot be explained by science.

I empathize with Clare's confusion, because I don't fully understand it myself. Would it make any sense if I said that my investigation of nature through literature and philosophy has been supplemental and separate from a foundation steeped in science? The best way I can describe it is to say I have become multidisciplinary in my environmental thinking when I should be interdisciplinary—and when push comes to shove, I slip back into my science-based ways.

None of this means I don't see the changes as positive. In the early 1980s, I was drawn to the first inklings of what was to become the ecological age. I wanted to write my PhD dissertation on Thoreau's philosophical views about leisure. The problem was that no professor, not in the social sciences or the humanities, could tell me how to approach the subject in a way that would be acceptable to a science-oriented dissertation committee. That being said, the comments from all of the professors, regardless of their fields, were revealing. The consensus was that I had a good idea, but if I wanted to get through a traditional social science graduate program without a ton of hassles, I should complete my formal training by doing a mainstream dissertation using an established methodology—and wait until after graduation to deviate too far from the way things are usually done. Thirty years later, one of my graduate students, with the help of a social scientist (me) and a professor from philosophy, successfully wrote her master's thesis on Thoreau's attitudes toward leisure.[7]

In another example within the university setting, biology professors at my university in the early 1990s fought tooth and nail against the establishment of an interdisciplinary environmental studies minor. Their sole argument was that the environmental studies curriculum was not science. More accurately, they lamented the minor was not entirely science, as there was a science component to the proposal. When the biologists' argument did not sway an undergraduate curriculum committee intermixed with faculty members from the humanities, some of the same biology professors announced they would not allow their advisees to take the new minor. Three decades later, biology faculty members, especially the younger professors, are some of the minor's strongest supporters, and one of them became the program's director.

There is a term that science-oriented resource managers used to use to goad environmentalists who identified with the spiritual and supernatural aspects of the nature–human relationship. The term is woo-woo. It is easy to imagine a technologically driven forester (probably old, probably male, definitely trained in the hard sciences) twirling a finger near his ear and muttering "woo-woo" under his breath when he heard new age nature lovers speak of myths, solstice celebrations, and a oneness with the cosmos. In one instance, I even heard it called, mostly in jest, not just woo-woo but "that voodoo woo-woo." Everyone in the room laughed at this clever turn of phrase, but it still pointed out the wide divide between potential allies. Today most resource managers are more open to new ideas, and the quirky verbiage of new age naturalism has been replaced by the more nuanced insights of the ecological age. I haven't heard the word "woo-woo" in a while-while.

I do not mean to overstate my reluctance to embrace the romantic side of the romantic–scientist continuum. I am making progress in that direction, and I credit two specific aspects of the ecological age for my gradual transformation. One is the inclusion of Tao philosophy in the discussion. The other is changes occurring within science itself.

The Yin and Yang of It

When I moved to Taiwan in 1991, I took language lessons at the Mandarin Training Center of National Taiwan Normal University. I also had the harebrained idea of translating the *Tao Te Ching* character by character as a way to learn written Chinese and simultaneously read the classic Taoist text in its original language. My efforts lasted all of six characters, when my interpretation of the famous opening line, "Dào kě dào fēi cháng dào" (道可道 非常道), came out as "The Tao that can be the Tao is not the Tao." It turns out my translation was not far off, but I did not know it at the time. Laotze was simply stating that even though the *Tao Te Ching* was words on the page, the true Tao cannot be put into words. At the same time I abandoned my *Tao Te Ching* translation project, I also learned that most Taiwanese (and most mainland Chinese for that matter) were not particularly Tao-like. "Oh no, Steve," as one of my Taiwanese friends told me, "we are in a constant state of Confucian."

My time in Taiwan taught me that, for a person who did not speak Mandarin fluently, it was easier to study the Tao in the English-speaking United States than in Asia. Two years in Taipei fueled my interest in Asian philosophy, but did little to satisfy it. That turned out to be okay, as Taoism became my bedtime reading once I moved back to Wisconsin.

Sitting up in bed alongside my Christian Taiwanese wife, I often struggled with an English version of *Chuangtze* while she read a Chinese translation of *The Holy Bible*. It was our personal cross-cultural exchange.

My investigation of the Tao helped me to understand my nature–human relationship in two significant ways. First of all, I realized I can be both part of and separate from the natural world at the same time. Alan Watts described it as humanity and nature being different, but of the same process.[8] Chung-ying Cheng, a pioneer in explaining the Tao to Westerners, wrote:

> Chinese philosophy focuses on man as the consummator of nature rather than man as the conqueror of nature, as a participant in nature rather than a predator of nature. Man as consummator of nature expresses continuously the beauty, truth, and goodness of nature, and articulates them in a moral or natural cultivation of human life or human nature.[9]

I could have learned the same lesson by reading Emerson and Thoreau, but as Dorothy discovered in Oz, we sometimes have to go to exotic places to discover what is in our own backyards.

Secondly, I came to realize many of the words used to describe the yin and the yang work equally well to explain the ecological age. The ecological age is not abandoning yangish science altogether, but recognizing the equally important role of yin-like romanticism. The differences between the two often are explained by listing their extremes side by side. This dichotomy certainly helped me to understand the yin and the yang, and it is not lost on me that it took a yangish either/or representation for me to comprehend a concept that is continuous and fluid.

Asking a person whether he or she is a romantic or a scientist is, in itself, a scientific yang approach to the question. Science, in this instance, is not a lab coat and a Bunsen burner. It is a way of thinking that breaks down and then categorizes things into their component parts. This is in contrast to looking at something holistically. How might I word the

romantic–scientist question without revealing my scientific bias so bla-
tantly? Let me try this: How do you best learn *about* nature? How do
you best learn *from* her? Looking at the ecological age through the yin
and the yang (see table 2) helped me to see I had made more progress
toward the romantic side of twenty-first-century thinking than I sometimes gave myself credit for. I may be dragging my feet when it comes to
embracing intuition and spirituality, but I am right there in terms of cy-
clic thinking, reflection, and process.

Table 2. How Do You Best Learn About Nature?
How Do You Best Learn From Her?

THE ROMANTIC (THE YIN)	THE SCIENTIST (THE YANG)
Immersion	Unintrusive observation from the outside
Synthesis	Analysis
Intuition	Logic and rationality
Spirituality	Sensory experience (what we see, hear . . .)
Holism	Categorization
Cyclic thinking	Linear thinking
Process	Results
Feelings	Facts
Reflection	Action
Qualitative insights	Quantitative insights
Feminine	Masculine
Poetry, literature, philosophy, theology, cultural anthropology (humanities)	Biology, chemistry, physics, physical geography (science)

The Blob of Life

At the same time I am consciously moving toward the middle ground between extreme yin and extreme yang, science is doing the same thing. The
ecological age has not merely elevated the importance of the humanities

in understanding the nature–human relationship; it also has changed science. The best example I can think of is the new tree of life, a model that depicts all species' evolutionary connection to each other.

To even call this new model a tree is a misnomer, as its design is not a tree at all. It is more an amoeba. I and all other baby boomers, at least those of us who were allowed to study evolution in school, had been taught to think of all life on the planet as a great tree. Microscopic creatures are the trunk (or maybe they are the roots; I don't recall), more advanced life-forms fill the branches, and at the very tiptop of the highest branch resides *Homo sapiens*. Although I don't remember it ever being explicitly expressed, the assumptions were (1) the life-forms in the trunk are stagnant (i.e., viruses and bacteria and single-cell organisms are done evolving, at least for the purposes of the model), (2) change takes place largely at the tips of the branches, and (3) human beings are evolution's finest accomplishment, maybe even its end game. One of my recollections about the tree of life was that no one was sure where to put mushrooms. Macroorganisms were divided into animals and photosynthetic plants, and fungi didn't fit either category.[10]

The new model depicting the evolution of life is not a tree. It is a single blob with three sub-blobs containing archaea, bacteria, and eukaryotes.[11] Evolutionary change occurs throughout the structure, not just at the tips. In fact, there are no tips. Animals with spines are such a minor element within the eukaryote sub-blob that some representations of the model don't list *Homo sapiens* at all. In other words, the new model so demotes the human species from the crowning achievement of evolution that humans hardly deserve mention.

Those of my generation grapple with this new depiction of the tree of life, and the struggle is more than reconciling errors in our long-held assumptions about the science. It is accepting *Homo sapiens* as a genetically insignificant outlier in 3.5 billion years of evolution. In other words, science within the ecological age requires a serious reassessment of humanity's place in the natural world.

I am writing this chapter sequestered in my house during the coronavirus pandemic. I hope by the time anyone has a chance to read these words, the crisis is over and humanity has used the pandemic to reassess, at least a little bit, its place in the biosphere. How much of the denial of the seriousness of COVID-19 has been a failure to admit that the most dynamic and arguably most powerful evolutionary changes on the planet are taking place at a microscopic level? A part of the ecological age is humility, and humility comes from a romantic interpretation of the latest insights of science. As Tucker and Swimme put it, "If scientific cosmology gives us understanding of the origins and unfolding of the universe, philosophical reflection on scientific cosmology gives us a sense of our place in the universe."[12]

Of the four continuums described in part III of this book, the romantic–scientist might be the most dynamic. For me, it also is the most confusing. There are times when I am immersed in my old scientific way of thinking and get frustrated with people who take romanticism to the extreme. A week later I find myself talking to the tomato plants in my garden. Anyone who maintains an open mind in nature will have experiences that cannot be explained logically or by any scientific means. As William R. Jordan, himself a biologist, stated, "Our relationship with the rest of nature, as with anything, is not really an equation or a problem to be solved. It is a mystery."[13]

21

The Restorer

There is a story being told around my hometown about two neighbors who live on a hill overlooking the La Crosse River Marsh. One neighbor sneaks into the marsh at night to wrap chicken wire around the trees nearest the water. He does it to protect the trees from beavers. The other neighbor also sneaks into the marsh. He goes there to undo the work of the first neighbor. He wants to help the beavers. I am not sure whether the story is true, but it doesn't really matter. Whether the tale of the two neighbors is fact or urban legend, the moral remains the same: Even people who want the best for nature may not agree on what to do.

LA CROSSE HAS TWO EXCEPTIONAL NATURAL AREAS WITHIN ITS CITY limits. One is the La Crosse River Marsh. This thousand-acre wetland extends the entire width of the city, all the way from the Mississippi River on the west to the bluffs on the east. It literally cuts the city in half, so much so that residents self-identify with which side of the marsh they live on. I am a Southsider; my house is less than a half mile from the southern edge of the marsh. It was a big deal when a shift in population distribution forced some of the kids living on the Southside to attend the Northside high school. The change in school boundaries was akin to forced bussing, although the reasons had more to do with available seats in the classroom than racial desegregation. My daughter was one of those students who got sent north. Even though we live only a mile from the Southside high school, she crossed the marsh every day to attend "Logan High, Pride of the Northside."

Most urban wetlands gradually get filled in to accommodate urban development. Here in La Crosse, our wetlands were actually created by development. The acreage where the marsh now resides is part of the La Crosse River floodplain. It's always been a low spot in the city, but was not always a four-season marsh. Historically, the area flooded every spring but was dry land most of the year. Gradually over the past century, a variety of dikes were built across the floodplain to raise roads and train tracks higher than the high-water mark. These earthen embankments unintentionally work as floodgates in reverse. They allow floodwaters into the low areas, but then hold some of the water back when it naturally would have receded. The trapped water collects in permanent pools, and the result is the largest urban marsh in the state of Wisconsin.

Two or three times a year I give a historical hike through the La Crosse River Marsh. There are a dozen good stories associated with the place, complete with Native American rendezvous, Polish immigrants raising geese for shipment to exclusive restaurants in Chicago, and Buffalo Bill Cody's association with La Crosse's turn-of-the-century eccentric, Doc Powell.

When I lead this particular hike, I often start by conducting an introductory activity at the trailhead. I hand every participant a slip of paper. Each slip lists one possible way for developing a marsh. It might say, "Fill in the marsh to create land for low-income housing" or "Build a golf course" or "Tear out the levees to return the marsh to its natural condition." One of the strips of paper reads, "Put in nineteenth-century streetlamps to create a romantic lovers' lane." Whenever I conducted this hike with my own students, I intentionally gave the lovers' lane piece of paper to the most rough-around-the-edges, gravelly voiced outdoorsman in the class. Everyone would laugh as he read it aloud. I do not tell the participants beforehand that all of the options are real. They were either an actual use of the La Crosse River Marsh in earlier times or a proposal for the marsh that had been seriously considered but not implemented.

I then ask the participants, through consensus, to line up the uses of the marsh in order from "best" to "worst." I have conducted this activity at least two dozen times, and the No. 1 "best" answer is always the same. Every single time the participants want to "leave the marsh as is."

The other wonderful natural area in La Crosse is an urban forest called Hixon Forest. One of my more memorable experiences in the forest was not hiking, but facilitating a small trail restoration project. Philosophy professor Sam Cocks asked if I could arrange a weekend ecological restoration project for the students in his environmental philosophy course. I told him a local conservation group was looking for volunteers to help close off rogue trails near the main trailhead in Hixon Forest. Rogue trails are paths formed when so many people take the same unauthorized shortcut that the foot traffic creates a trail where a trail should not be. Often these makeshift routes bypass long switchbacks, which means they accomplish exactly what responsible trail construction is designed to avoid—that is, eroding the hillside by sending hikers straight up and down steep and unstable terrain. The most common way to close off rogue trails is to fill in any washouts with dirt and leaves, then pile so much brush on top of the washout that it is easier for hikers and/or mountain bikers to stay on the established path than to take the rogue. Sam liked the project, and a work day was arranged.

I made the assumption Sam was just looking for an opportunity to get his students outside. After he and his students had spent weeks in a classroom discussing humankind's relationship with the natural world, I figured he wanted his students to get their hands dirty. In this regard, I was partially right. He did want to get his students outdoors, but he also specifically wanted them to work on a restoration project. I didn't know it when Sam asked for help, but ecological restoration is an acknowledged subarea within the broader discipline of environmental philosophy. Sam had made ecological restoration a major theme in his course that particular semester and wanted his students to experience it firsthand.

Professional trail builder Chad DuChateau supervised Sam, his students, and me through a full morning's work along Hixon Forest's Vista Trail. In addition to removing rogue trails, we did repair work on the designated trail where it intersected with the rogues. With other work crews I've been on, we would do manual labor for anywhere between two to eight hours, receive a quick "thank you" from the organizers, and then be on our way. Sam, ever the philosophy professor, was not finished with his students once they'd taken off their hardhats and work gloves. He'd brought lunch and had everyone sit together on the ground to eat and reflect upon the morning.

The first point Sam wanted to make was that not all conservation work is restorative. Ecological restoration, by definition, returns a resource to a more natural state. Harvesting prairie seed from an established prairie for redistribution elsewhere is ecological restoration. Helping with a prescribed burn on that very same prairie is ecological restoration. Erosion abatement, reforestation, riparian repair, and the removal of invasive species are all examples of ecological restoration. These actions attempt to return a piece of nature to a more pristine condition.

There are, however, equally worthwhile conservation projects that have minimal impact on the resource itself. Litter cleanup might fall into this category. So too might the installation of benches, interpretive signs, and other hiker amenities. One of the most interesting conservation projects I've ever worked on was the construction of a large, roofed kiosk at a trailhead. When finished, I thought the kiosk contained information important to hikers (e.g., a map of the various loop trails and a warning to watch out for poison ivy), but the kiosk's impact on Mother Nature was negligible.

Because the manual labor with Sam's philosophy class had been trail maintenance, Sam turned the discussion to whether trail construction and trail maintenance constituted ecological restoration. In the opinion of the students, cutting trail into undisturbed landscapes did not qualify. New trails expand opportunities for recreation and education, but they do not make a piece of nature more pristine. The students concluded that removing rogue trails was ecological restoration, but its impact on the natural environment was not significant.

I mentioned to the students that a landscape architect who designed trails for the Iowa State Parks once told me his job was not to make nature accessible. It was to redirect park users away from natural areas that were best left undisturbed. His favorite projects were boardwalks with railings, not because they provided the most interesting design challenges but because the finished product corralled park visitors into a confined space and prevented them from damaging "his" parks.[1] In his mind, trail construction done right was ecological restoration.

One of Sam's students asked, "What difference does it make whether our work today was ecological restoration? Good work in the outdoors is good work. Isn't that enough?" I had been thinking exactly the same thing, but as soon as the words came out of the young woman's mouth, I realized Sam's question about trails had been a setup.

"It matters only if we care why we do the work," replied Sam. "If our only goal is to make nature more natural, then we should only take on projects that are clearly restorative. If, however, our goals are broader, then it might not matter so much. Having said that, all of the other reasons I can think of for doing conservation work are to benefit people more than nature. In other words, they are anthropocentric and not biocentric. Most trail work, for example, benefits the human visitors more than it does the plants and animals."

The students picked up on the subject immediately. "And the goal of the work today," one of them said, "was to apply the stuff from class to a real situation. The intent was more to get us thinking than it was to improve the forest."

"So did the work do that?" asked Sam. "What did you get out of the morning?" The students concluded that the work, whether or not it was restorative, enhanced their connection with nature, taught them a little about ecology and trail construction, offered them a chance to work alongside like-minded environmentalists, and provided a sense of accomplishment. One student said he wouldn't wantonly step off-trail anymore. Another observed that she would remember this particular weekend out of all of her weekends that semester as the one she did a bit of community service.[2]

Sam then asked whether the students knew anything about the history of Hixon Forest. When none did, he explained that Hixon Forest, like the nearby La Crosse River Marsh, was not an entirely natural ecosystem. The marsh, he said, came about because of the construction of levees. Hixon Forest, on the other hand, came about because of a land purchase made over a hundred years ago. Wealthy La Crosse resident Irene Hixon bought the bluffs and coulees east of the city as a way to stop plans for a large-scale quarry operation. At the time, the land was mostly meadows and goat prairie.[3] Only after Mrs. Hixon bought the land and let it go fallow did the trees move in.

"We sometimes think," Sam said, "that ecological restoration is an attempt to return a piece of land to its original natural condition. That is not always the case. Ecological restoration improves a resource's ecological health, but the benchmark for a restoration project is not necessarily the resource's pre-European settlement condition. As often as not, the goal is to return a resource to a condition recalled by the people pushing for the restoration. People remember what the forest or the marsh or grassland looked like when they were kids, and they want it to be that way again.

"Such is the case with Hixon Forest. No one, to my knowledge, has ever suggested that Hixon Forest be returned to meadow. What people want is to keep the area as a forest, but return it to the way the forest was fifty years ago. Currently the resource has problems. There are too many deer, the understory is devoid of vegetation because of overgrazing by those deer, and the ages of the trees are pretty much all the same. Yet even though people agree on what the problems are, they cannot agree on the solutions.

"Take, for example, the age of the trees. Most of the trees in Hixon Forest are the very trees that established themselves when Irene Hixon first bought the property. Most are eastern deciduous hardwoods. This means that all of the trees are mature, and some species, especially the black locust and silver maples, are overmature and dying at an increasingly rapid rate. This has led to a difference of opinion as to the appropriate human action.

"One group believes limited logging is necessary. Dying trees are a safety hazard, and they must be removed before a tree falls on somebody. Additionally, clearcutting small plots within the forest would create open space and a more vibrant understory. It would produce a forest with trees of varying age and species. It would replace the uniform forest that now exists. And while revenue from a logging operation is not justification for cutting down trees in an urban forest, it is a bonus. A continuous income stream from selective cutting could be used to make improvements to the forest that the city government cannot afford.

"Then there is an anti-logging group. These people also worry about too many deer and too little understory, but they think these problems are a result of repeated human interference. They don't see how continuing down the misguided path of constant intervention is a good solution. In their minds, Hixon Forest could be a rare urban forest where nature is left to its own devices. Certain animals, especially some species of birds, require deep and undisturbed forests to thrive. Many of these creatures need dying trees in the heart of the forest for both their homes and as a breeding ground for the insects upon which they feed.[4] To these anti-loggers, a climax forest is a natural stage in succession, and mature trees, both healthy and dying, are part of a flourishing ecosystem.

"This debate is, I think, an example where environmental philosophy has practical implications. One group believes that Hixon Forest is a disturbed area, and only intentional steps by knowledgeable resource managers can repair it. Another group, also seeking what is best for the forest, believes Hixon Forest has been repeatedly mismanaged, so humans should just get out of the way and allow the forest to heal itself. This is not a conflict between developers and preservationists. This is a disagreement between two groups of knowledgeable environmentalists who both want what's best for the forest. One side believes people need to step in to correct their past mistakes. The other side thinks it is arrogant of humans to claim they know what nature needs.

"And here's the kicker. Some of the people who believe nature should be left alone still volunteer for restoration projects. Some of you might have been one of those people today. They say nature should be left alone, yet they go ahead and make incremental changes anyway. Restorative actions are not absolutely one way or the other, but how do we decide when to get involved and when to step aside?

"Today we eliminated rogue trails from a section of Hixon Forest, and we all feel like we made the area a little more natural. Would it make any difference if I told you that a couple of the trails we removed today were started by deer? People stepped in behind the deer and packed down the ground more than deer alone would have—but because of our well-intentioned interference, deer now have to find a different place to walk. Did you ever think that trying to do the ecologically right thing would be so complicated?"

The Key May Be the Questions
Rather Than the Answers

As Sam linked the general principles of ecological restoration specifically to Hixon Forest, I was reminded of an old essay by John Dewey.[5] In "The Duties and Responsibilities of the Teaching Profession," Dewey wrote about teachers finding the right balance between teaching students to think independently and encouraging them to respect the norms of society. If democracy was going to work, claimed Dewey, teachers must simultaneously help students to become both cooperative members of society and independent thinkers willing to question the values of the local community when those values seem wrong. He claimed, however, that he could not offer any one-size-fits-all tips for finding the right balance between these two important, but potentially conflicting, objectives. Every community, every educator, and every educational system has its own unique features, so teachers have to figure out for themselves the appropriate level of teacher autonomy. Instead of providing specific recommendations, Dewey listed ten questions educators might ask themselves to better understand their own position on this important issue. As one example, Dewey asked teachers whether they believed criticism of the existing social order should be permitted in the classroom and, if so, what form should it take.

A hands-on versus a hands-off approach to ecological restoration is analogous to Dewey's educational conundrum in that there is no single best solution. Each restoration project has its own quirks, and thoughtful environmentalists have to wade through multiple options to find the one that works best for them in the specific situation. To help with this sometimes difficult process, there are several good questions individuals can ask themselves to clarify their own views. The following is a list of ten questions about ecological restoration Sam helped me compile.[6] Some came up during his discussion with the students that day. Some did not.

1. What tasks do you consider ecological restoration? What tasks do you consider good conservation work, but not ecological restoration? What distinctions do you make between the two?

2. For the restoration projects in your community, what would a successful result look like?

3. If ecological restoration in your community is returning a resource to an earlier time, what era is the target? What is the level of naturalness being sought?

4. Can humans ever improve upon nature? Conversely, do you sometimes think people should stop intervening and just let nature take its course? Explain.

5. Is there value in demonstration plots? For example, what is the value of a postage stamp–sized prairie within acres and acres of corn and soybeans?[7]

6. Do you consider restored ecosystems to be natural? Does it matter to you whether a particular nature reserve was created by Mother Nature or re-created by human intervention? Explain.

7. Why do you volunteer for ecological restoration projects?

8. What is your opinion of restoration projects with very little restorative value, their primary purpose being either symbolic (e.g., Earth Day litter cleanups) or beneficial to the people doing the work (e.g., a Scout troop volunteering to repair a section of hiking trail)?

9. What is your opinion of people who travel halfway around the world to conduct ecological restoration (e.g., to help newly hatched sea turtles reach the sea) when there is much to be done locally?

10. How is your community service in nature different from your play in nature?

On most days I do not care whether a worthwhile project is ecological restoration or simply necessary conservation work. Just as the student in Sam's class pointed out, good work outdoors is good work. After a day of it, my back aches, my hands are either callused or blistered, and I feel like I've made a small positive impact. Well-intentioned conservation projects that benefit recreationists strike me as being as meaningful as projects that primarily benefit the resource. Both may even be part of what Thomas Berry called "The Great Work." He was referring to the conscious steps required of humankind to put the ecological age into practice. He wrote:

> The Great Work... is to carry out the transition from a period of human devastation of the Earth to a period when humans would be present to the planet in a *mutually* beneficial manner [italics mine].[8]

While I don't usually care whether a conservation work project is restorative, I really enjoyed the debate Sam introduced on the trail. When he eloquently brought to light the distinctions between ecological restoration and other conservation work, he meshed academic environmental philosophy with hard science in a way I've never been able to do—and in doing so he elevated environmental philosophy above intellectual nitpicking. Personally I am not sure how Sam tolerates the minutiae within his own discipline, but I have to assume he skims through the reams of esoteric rambling in search of the occasional gem. For every half dozen pointless rehashes of whether *A Sand County Almanac* is real philosophy or pseudo-philosophy, environmental philosophy introduces an insight or two that forces us to question our own values and beliefs.

Epilogue

Peter Matthiessen is one of my favorite non-fiction writers, and I think his best book is The Snow Leopard. *It is about a Himalayan trek he took in the early 1970s. Upon Matthiessen's death, his son Alex retraced the journey made famous in his dad's book.[1] As a boy, Alex lost his mother to cancer, and it was only two years after her death that the elder Matthiessen took off for Nepal. I have no idea whether Dad felt any guilt about temporarily leaving his son while the boy might still be grieving, but I am certain he would have been proud had he known that one of the long-term effects of* The Snow Leopard *was Alex eventually pursuing his own Himalayan adventure. If only all of us could leave a comparable impact upon our children.*

I MENTIONED IN THE PREFACE TO THIS BOOK THAT I WROTE IT AS A SEries of letters to Clare. Obviously the chapters were not written in letter form, but each anecdote was, as I wrote the original draft with pen and paper, a story being told to her. Maybe the best way to finish this book is to do away with the pretense that my primary audience is the general public and actually make this last chapter what it really is: a closing letter to my daughter.

Dear Clare,

When I started this book, you were trying to figure out what you would do after high school. As I write this final chapter, you are only days away from graduating from college. The years I worked on this book have been time well spent, even though I've pretty much ended up where I started—thinking it is not as important for people to understand their personal environmental philosophies as it is for them to spend time outdoors.

And when it comes to time in nature, I worry a little bit. I do not worry so much about me, but about you. I am retired now and have set aside time each week for playing outside. In the years since retirement, I've spent more time in the woods and on the river than I ever did when I had a job. You, on the other hand, are just starting your adult life. If you are like me when I was almost done with my undergraduate degree, you are thinking that you will suddenly have more free time once you finish college. Unfortunately, and I am serious when I say it is unfortunate, life does not work that way. You will soon be busier than ever. I know that you enjoy hiking and paddling. I know you have a lifelong commitment to protecting the planet. I am less certain whether these qualities will translate into frequent nature-related outings. You are a responsible person, and I can easily imagine you putting family, friends, and work above your outdoor pursuits. This is as it should be, but not to the point where it places outdoor recreation on a back burner that is never attended to. Make sure you make time for the outdoors. I can't make it plainer than that.

Whenever I led extended canoe trips with my students, I would always put ashore one last time a mile upstream of the takeout. I'd gather everyone together in a circle and invite each student to speak his or her mind about the trip. After everyone else had spoken, I got the final word. Sometimes a certain event on a particular trip would require that I talk about it, but more often than not I'd used the following general closing. What I told them might also apply to you:

> I already know what will probably happen next. All of you will get home from this trip on a high, excited to tell your spouse, your boy-friend, your girlfriend, your parents, or your roommate about the

wonderful time you had. We did just have a very good trip. You will tell those close to you that time in nature is better than time in the city. But then the high will fade. You will return to your classes and your jobs, your cell phones, and your computers. By the end of the week, this trip will get filed away alongside other adventures you've had. This is not a criticism. I will do the same thing, even though I consciously remind myself not to. Right now you might be able to tell yourself that nature is real and urban life is not. In a week, that thought will reverse itself. City life again will become real, and our paddle together will become a fond memory. All I can ask is for you to remember how good you feel right now and realize how easy it will be to generate those feelings again. Nature should be experienced often, big trips at least once a year and day outings several times a month. I did not bring you on this canoe trip for this trip alone. I took you on this trip to encourage you to spend time outdoors after this trip. Don't forget how good you feel right now and how relaxed you are. This trip is unique, and a couple of memorable things happened. That does not mean the next outing won't also be special. You need to encounter nature again and again.

Clare, you know that A Sand County Almanac *is one of my favorite books. You probably don't know that its last sentence has guided me for most of my teaching career. The sentence reads, "Recreational development is a job not of building roads into lovely country, but of building receptivity into the still unlovely human mind."[2] I can never hope to finish this letter to you with anything nearly as profound as Leopold's closing words, but I can borrow Leopold's literary cadence to make my own final statement:*

> *Environmental awareness is a lifelong pursuit not merely of studying ecology and reading the great nature writers, but of going into the wild and reflecting on our own experiences in the natural world.*

Love your mom, love me, and love nature,
Dad[3]

Acknowledgments

I AM NOT GOING TO THANK BY NAME THE MANY FRIENDS, TEACHERS, family members, and students who taught me things about nature. If I did, I would later be haunted by the people I left out. Some of them are mentioned by name in the stories of this book.

Ed Grant, Mony Cunningham, Sara Tipler, Anna DeMers, CJ Jackson, Stefan Smith, and Sam Cocks all received early versions of the manuscript and provided valuable feedback. Ed had first shot at many of the essays, and his early reviews were especially useful. Mony added a full eight months to the project when she told me that the original version of part III did not work, but she was right.

A significant number of people at Purdue University Press helped to improve the quality of this book. I especially want to thank Justin Race, Andrea Gapsch, Katherine Purple, Kelley Kimm, and Chris Brannan. My experience with this group of people has been wholly positive.

Manyu has supported me in my writing for thirty years, even when I took leaves of absence from my various teaching positions so I could write full-time. Her first language is Mandarin, so she does not read a lot of books in English—but she reads mine. Clare, even though she didn't know it at the time, has been my muse on this book.

Notes

Preface

1. In the opinion of many environmentalists, myself included, Aldo Leopold's *A Sand County Almanac* is one of the three most important books in American environmental literature (the other two being *Silent Spring* and *Walden*). First published in 1949, it did not become popular until the late 1960s and early 1970s. The land ethic, a major theme in the last third of the book, remains a cornerstone of contemporary American environmental thought. For those who have not read *A Sand County Almanac*, the pages of my book offer glimpses of the great work, but anyone serious about articulating a personal environmental philosophy will want to go straight to the source.

2. Leopold's game management program at the University of Wisconsin eventually became wildlife ecology, which then merged with forestry to become the Department of Forest and Wildlife Ecology.

3. Stegner made the observation several years after my stint at the University of Wisconsin, but the principle still applies. Wallace Stegner, "The Legacy of Aldo Leopold," in *Companion to A Sand County Almanac*, ed. J. Baird Callicott (Madison: University of Wisconsin Press, 1987), 233–45.

4. My college copy of *A Sand County Almanac* is the Sierra Club/Ballantine paperback, not the original Oxford University Press publication. There now are more than two editions of the book available, but the versions from 1949 and 1966 remain the standards. They are Aldo Leopold, *A Sand County Almanac and Sketches Here and There* (London: Oxford University Press, 1949), and Aldo Leopold, *A Sand County Almanac: With Essays on Conservation from Round River* (New York: Sierra Club/Ballantine, 1966). The Sierra Club/Ballantine paperback contains a handful of essays not in the Oxford University Press publication.

5. Kenn Maly, "A Sand County Almanac: Through Anthropogenic to Ecogenic Thinking," in *Rethinking Nature: Essays in Environmental Philosophy*, ed. Bruce V. Foltz and Robert Frodeman (Bloomington, IN: Indiana University Press, 2004), 289–301.

6. Stephen King, *On Writing: A Memoir of the Craft* (New York: Scribner, 2000).

7. An academic environmental philosopher would not consider this book philosophy at all, but see it as pseudo-philosophy coming from a well-intentioned amateur. I would agree with this assessment. Still, a person who understands his or her relationship to the natural world really has all he or she needs in terms of an environmental foundation.

Introduction

1. *A Private Universe* (Cambridge, MA: Harvard-Smithsonian Center for Astrophysics, 1987), https://vimeo.com/113349804.

2. Even though I describe my dad as a libertarian environmentalist, I really don't understand what this means. If I had to guess, I'd say it might be that a government should provide only three things: a strong military, good educational opportunities, and a sound infrastructure—with a healthy natural ecosystem qualifying as infrastructure. My dad and I got along, but we didn't talk politics much.

3. John Dewey, *Experience and Education* (New York: Touchstone, 1938).

Chapter 1

1. Paul Smith, "Wisconsin Turkey Flock a Wild Success Story," *Press-Gazette* (Green Bay, WI), November 25, 2017, https://www.jsonline.com/story/sports/columnists/paul-smith/2017/11/22/smith-wisconsin-turkey-flock-wild-success-story/881522001/. Also found Wisconsin Department of Natural Resources, *Ecology of Wild Turkeys in Wisconsin*, https://www.wistatedocuments.org/digital/collection/p267601coll4/id/10526.

2. Dan Egan, *The Death and Life of the Great Lakes* (New York: W. W. Norton, 2017), 68.

3. On Interstate 90, the numbers on the mile markers get smaller as motorists travel east to west. Our drive from the Shack took us from mile marker 92 to mile marker 5.

4. Except for the first Earth Day and the bear in Myrick Park, I did not know the dates of these events when they came to mind. I had to look up the dates after I got home. The Google search for the exact years was useful in that I learned things about the events I'd either forgotten or perhaps never knew.

5. In the years since this trip, both Pier 1 and Shopko have gone bankrupt. Some of the chain restaurants have closed (Old Country Buffet, Ground Round), only to have others move into the available space (Chipotle, Noodles and Company).

6. National Park Service interpretive programs, especially the ones at their historical sites, try to link historical events with the daily lives of the visitors. The NPS calls it meaningful interpretation. David L. Larsen, Ed., *Meaningful Interpretation: How to Connect Hearts and Minds to Places, Objects, and Other Resources* (Washington, PA: Eastern National, 2003).

7. "Rest! cries the chief sawyer, and we pause for breath" are the words embossed on the small plaque that commemorates the Good Oak.

Chapter 2

1. The most southern dam on the Upper Mississippi River is just upstream of St. Louis. From there, all the way to the Gulf of Mexico, the land is fairly flat and the change in elevation is gradual. Locks and dams are no longer needed to facilitate barge traffic.

2. The high waters that year lasted until the Fourth of July, and some of the flooded trees eventually died. They would have handled having their roots submerged for a short period of time, but could not tolerate having them underwater for months on end.

3. Henry D. Thoreau, *The Illustrated Walden* (Princeton: Princeton University Press, 1973), 333.

4. Stephen Jay Gould, *The Panda's Thumb: More Reflections in Natural History* (New York: W. W. Norton, 1980), 59–68.

Chapter 3

1. The album is *It Takes A Year*. William Ackerman is a musician on Windham Hill Records. In the 1980s and '90s, Windham Hill produced albums of quiet jazz by guitarists and pianists.

2. Henry David Thoreau, "Wild Apples," in *The Selected Works of Thoreau*, ed. Walter Harding (Boston: Houghton Mifflin, 1975), 726.

3. Belden C. Lane, *Backpacking with the Saints: Wilderness Hiking as Spiritual Practice* (New York: Oxford University Press, 2015), 14.

Chapter 4

1. Henry D. Thoreau, *The Illustrated Walden* (Princeton: Princeton University Press, 1973), 212.

2. These mixed feelings about fishing were presented most explicitly in the *Walden* chapter "Higher Laws." He wrote, "I have found repeatedly, of late years, that I cannot fish without falling a little in self-respect." Henry David Thoreau, *Walden* (New York: Book of the Month Club, 1996), 283.

3. As I think about fish on a stringer, I realize I never brought fish home when I was on my bicycle. In the 1960s, the waters around my home in Green Bay, Wisconsin, were so polluted no one ate the fish. I only used a stringer when I was with my dad well away from the effluents of the paper mills. I think the fish in the lower bay of Green Bay now are as safe to eat as fish caught elsewhere, but it is permanently imprinted on my brain that the fish there are laced with really bad stuff.

4. Henry David Thoreau, Walden (New York: Book of the Month Club, 1996), 119.

5. Other technological advances that distinguish motorboat fishing from canoe fishing include fish finders, GPS units, trolling motors, electric anchor hoists, and circulating live wells.

6. *The Compleat Angler* is a book about fishing written by Izaak Walton in the 1600s.

Chapter 5

I titled this chapter "A Person's Leisure Time." One of the chapters in the Sierra Club/Ballantine version of *A Sand County Almanac* that does not appear in the Oxford University edition is titled "A Man's Leisure Time."

1. Aristotle frequently wrote about leisure. Starting points for anyone interested in the Aristotelian view of leisure include Aristotle, *Ethics*, trans. J. A. K. Thomson (Middlesex: Penguin, 1976), Book I, ch. 2, and Book IX, ch. 9, and

Aristotle, *Politics*, trans. Ernest Barker (Oxford: Oxford University Press, 1948), Book VIII, ch. v–vii.

2. The classic work about conspicuous consumption and opulent leisure is Thorstein Veblen's *The Theory of the Leisure Class* (Oxford: Oxford University Press, 2007).

3. Aristotle referred only to "free" men, not women, in his discussions about leisure.

4. Aristotle, *Ethics*, trans. J. A. K. Thomson (Middlesex: Penguin, 1976), 1179a.

5. Aldo Leopold, *A Sand County Almanac: With Essays on Conservation from Round River* (New York: Sierra Club/Ballantine, 1966), 181.

6. John Muir, *The Wilderness World of John Muir*, ed. Edwin Way Teale (Boston: Houghton Mifflin, 1954), 320.

7. Henry David Thoreau, "Life Without Principle," in *The Selected Works of Thoreau*, ed. Walter Harding (Boston: Houghton Mifflin, 1975), 809.

8. Richard Louv, *Last Child in the Woods: Saving Our Children from Nature-Deficit Disorder* (Chapel Hill, NC: Algonquin Books, 2005), 120.

9. Tiziano Terzani, *A Fortune-Teller Told Me: Earthbound Travels in the Far East* (New York: Three Rivers Press, 1997).

10. Terzani's fishermen story reminds me of the hypothetical question "If you worked at an unpleasant job that paid $1 million/day, how long would you work?"

Chapter 6

1. In a nutshell, *The Image* is about (1) our individual picture of the world and (2) the ways teachers might constructively affect that picture. Kenneth E. Boulding, *The Image: Knowledge in Life and Society* (Ann Arbor: University of Michigan Press, 1961).

2. As to the relative absence of fiction, I want to point out that this list is the books I think my students should read before they die. It is not a list of my favorite books, which is not the same thing. *Catch-22*, *Trout Fishing in America*, *The Razor's Edge*, and *Shoeless Joe* are among my favorite books. I just don't feel the need to recommend them to anyone else.

3. Joseph Sax was still alive when my friend made this comment, but his in-

ference that my list lacked anything written in the previous thirty years was accurate.

4. Joseph Sax, *Mountains Without Handrails: Reflections on the National Parks* (Ann Arbor: University of Michigan Press, 1980), 47–48.

5. This phrase could have come from Sax, but came from E. O. Wilson. E. O. Wilson, "The 8 Million Species We Don't Know," *New York Times Sunday Review*, March 3, 2018, https://www.nytimes.com/2018/03/03/opinion/sunday/species-conservation-extinction.html.

6. Some readers might react to this sentiment by asking, "Why not teach kids to dance wildly in the moonlight with the tree spirits?" Anyone who would ask that question has never had to explain to parents how their kids went on a naturalist-led hike in the redwoods and encountered nature lovers who considered clothing to be optional. This happened to me. Fortunately the nude people were not my staff but were bare-assed hikers who'd wandered in from an organic farming conference being held at a second conference grounds just down the road from us. My mind immediately went into damage control mode when a group of sixth graders ran up to me after a hike one day and excitedly exclaimed, "Steve, Steve, guess what we saw in the woods today. We saw naked people!"

7. The pertinent passage reads, "As I came home through the woods with my string of fish, trailing my pole, it being now quite dark, I caught a glimpse of a woodchuck stealing across my path, and felt a strange thrill of savage delight, and was strongly tempted to seize and devour him raw; not that I was hungry then, except for that wildness which he represented." It comes from the opening to my favorite chapter of *Walden*, "Higher Laws." Henry D. Thoreau, *The Illustrated Walden* (Princeton: Princeton University Press, 1973), 210.

8. The pertinent passage reads, "For the first time, perhaps, since that land emerged from the waters of geologic ages, a human face was set toward it with love and yearning.... Then the Genius of the Divide, the great, free spirit which breathes across it, must have bent lower than it ever bent to a human will before. The history of every country begins in the heart of a man or a woman." Willa Cather, *O Pioneers!* (Boston: Houghton Mifflin, 1913, 1941), 65.

Chapter 7

1. Zygodactyl is a term I knew neither as a five-year-old, nor as a sixty-seven-year-old. I had to look it up. It refers to bird feet with two toes pointing forward and two toes pointing back. Whereas three toes forward, one toe back are best for perching, a zygodactyl arrangement is better for glomming onto vertical tree trunks (or, in the case of owls, grasping prey).

2. Stephen Bacon, *The Conscious Use of Metaphor in Outward Bound* (Denver: Colorado Outward Bound School, 1983).

Chapter 8

1. Steve Van Matre, *Earth Education: A New Beginning* (Warrensville, IL: Institute for Earth Education, 1990), 78–79.

2. When I applied for the naturalist position in Northern California's Jones Gulch, I'd never seen a redwood forest before. By the time I arrived at the environmental education center for the interview, I didn't care whether I got the naturalist job. I would have worked in the kitchen washing dishes. I was disappointed when I did not initially get a job offer. Three months later, however, a new position opened up, and I was hired the second time around.

Chapter 9

1. BWCA is the Boundary Waters Canoe Area. Officially it is the BWCAW (Boundary Waters Canoe Area Wilderness), but no one I know uses the longer acronym.

2. Each person has his or her own definition of the word "wilderness." For some people, a state park is wilderness. For others, nothing short of a half million acres without a road qualifies. Designated wilderness, on the other hand, is an official government designation. It is a federal or state agency establishing official boundaries and declaring everything within those boundaries a wilderness area.

3. James Lee Burke, *Robicheaux* (New York: Simon & Schuster, 2018), 43.

4. This quote is famous because Aldo Leopold cited it in *A Sand County Almanac*. Leopold wrote it as "Where nameless men by nameless rivers wan-

der and in strange valleys die strange deaths alone." The original source is Service's poem "To the Man of the High North." Robert Service, *Collected Poems of Robert Service* (New York: G. P. Putnam's Sons, 1940), 77.

5. Patricia Hampl, *The Art of the Wasted Day* (New York: Viking, 2018), 31.

6. Ibid., 240.

7. Although my Mandarin should have been better, many of my Taiwanese students welcomed the opportunity to work with me in English. They dreamed of attending graduate school in the US and saw me as a convenient, non-threatening test of their language skills.

Chapter 12

1. Helen Kopnina, "Evaluating Education for Sustainable Development (ESD): Using Ecocentric and Anthropocentric Attitudes Toward the Sustainable Development (EAATSD) Scale," *Environment, Development and Sustainability* 15 (2013): 607–23.

2. One significant exception to this generalization is the retired people who work as volunteer naturalists.

3. Gary Snyder, "Buddhism and the Possibilities of a Planetary Culture," in Bill Devall and George Sessions, *Deep Ecology: Living as if Nature Mattered* (Layton, UT: Gibbs M. Smith, 1985), 251–53.

Chapter 13

1. Black bear attacks are unusual, but not unheard of. On average, 1 person a year in North America dies from a bear attack. This is compared to 150 per year who die from hitting deer with their cars. About 20 people per year, mostly ranchers, are killed by domestic cattle.

2. There is disagreement about the best way to dispose of fish carcasses in the backcountry. Purists say to hike them out, but to me, keeping a week's worth of stinky fish guts in my trash is an unreasonable expectation. Burying them is one option, but buried fish parts often get dug up by various animals. My preferred method is to put them on a rock for the gulls and pelicans, even though this goes against the general minimum impact policy of not feeding wildlife. Throwing them in the water may be the worst possible choice.

Unless turtles find the bones and entrails, they can remain on the bottom of the lake for months.

3. It is also doubtful that the local residents were asked their opinions about the tourism development. Most likely the locals who benefit financially from tourism welcome the visitors, but those who do not benefit would prefer to turn back the clock.

Chapter 14

1. Aldo Leopold, A *Sand County Almanac: With Essays on Conservation from Round River* (New York: Sierra Club/Ballantine, 1966), 223.

2. United States Geological Survey. USGS is the primary scientific branch of the Department of the Interior. Near my home in La Crosse, Wisconsin, the agency studies the Upper Mississippi River.

3. I do not exaggerate when I call it a wonder of the world. Dujiangyan is a UNESCO World Heritage Site.

4. Henry D. Thoreau, *The Illustrated Walden* (Princeton: Princeton University Press, 1973), 298.

5. Mark Twain, *A Connecticut Yankee in King Arthur's Court* (New York: Washington Square Press, 1977).

6. "Kip" is the Laotian monetary system. $1 US dollar = ฿27 Thai baht = ₭8500 Laotian kip. You do the math.

7. The official name of Laos is the Laotian People's Democratic Republic.

8. A long-tailed outboard motor means the propeller is not tight alongside the engine. Instead it is on a long extension bar and trails the boat by ten to twenty feet. This is for shallow water. Whereas a conventional propeller can be as much as two feet below the surface of the water, the prop on a long-tailed outboard is down as little as six inches.

9. Readers may have eaten Asian catfish (aka iridescent shark or iridescent shark catfish) and not even known it. Here in North America, it is marketed and sold as swai. There are two things to know about swai. One, the fish sold as swai is *not* the same fish as the critically endangered Mekong giant catfish. Two, swai sold in American supermarkets is usually farm-raised in Vietnam and likely full of chemicals. These chemicals not only accumulate in the meat,

but also dissolve in fish farm wastewater and are released into the Vietnamese ecosystem.

Chapter 15

1. Richard Louv, *Last Child in the Woods: Saving Our Children from Nature-Deficit Disorder* (Chapel Hill, NC: Algonquin Books, 2005).

2. Aldo Leopold, "The Role of Wildlife in a Liberal Arts Education," in *River of the Mother of God and Other Essays by Aldo Leopold*, eds. Susan L. Flader and J. Baird Callicott (Madison: University of Wisconsin Press, 1991), 301–5.

3. The COVID-19 pandemic has shown that large lecture-based courses can be taught online, so general education courses may be drifting even further away from hands-on learning.

4. If there is anything countering a move toward even more large lecture college courses, it might be the recent trend toward first-year seminars. In such classes, innovative professors often take small numbers of students into the field.

5. To make a point, I may have exaggerated Louv's views on unsupervised play in nature. When he made suggestions for addressing what he called nature-deficit disorder, his very first recommendation was for parents to take their kids outside. Louv stressed unstructured play as much as unsupervised play.

6. The Trempealeau National Wildlife Refuge became a refuge only after no one could figure out a way to make money off the resource. The main feature of the refuge is a series of artificial ponds, originally dug to drain a large marsh for agriculture. The project failed miserably as the area flooded anyway, but the ponds became ideal rest stops for migrating waterfowl along the Mississippi Flyway. The refuge now is one of the best places in the Upper Midwest to observe white pelicans and, in the autumn, ducks, swans, and geese.

7. Kenneth E. Boulding, *The Image: Knowledge in Life and Society* (Ann Arbor: University of Michigan Press, 1956).

8. Dan Egan, interview by Jeffrey Brown, "'Great Lakes' Author Dan Egan Answers Your Questions," *PBS News Hour*, April 30, 2018, https://www.pbs .org/newshour/show/great-lakes-author-dan-egan-answers-your-questions.

Chapter 16

1. The mention of elephant dung might seem out of place here, but it is one of my once-in-a-lifetime memories. Hiking Thailand's Khao Yai National Park, the banyan trees and other exotic vegetation were different from anything I'd ever seen before, but it was piles of elephant poop in the middle of the trail that told me I wasn't in Wisconsin anymore.

2. A primary purpose of the story in chapter 11 about sunrise at Yushan was to point out that the magic of nature does sometime happen in crowds.

3. Ralph Waldo Emerson, *Nature* (Boston: James Munroe and Company, 1949).

4. I told this same story in a previous book. Steven Simpson, *Rediscovering Dewey: A Reflection on Independent Thinking* (Bethany, OK: Wood N Barnes, 2011).

Chapter 17

1. The origin of the name Hetch Hetchy is fuzzy. One theory is that the first non–Native American to enter the valley watched the indigenous people roast a grain called hatch hatchie and named the valley after it.

2. John Muir, "The Hetch Hetchy Valley," *Boston Weekly Transcript*, March 25, 1873, https://vault.sierraclub.org/john_muir_exhibit/writings/muir_hh_boston_25mar1873.aspx.

3. "Lapping tamed waters" is a paraphrase from Gene Rose's article "The Ghosts of Hetch-Hetchy" (*Yosemite Association* 56, no. 3 [1994]: 10–11).

4. The United States was the first country in the world to have national parks. Yellowstone was the very first national park, but the enabling legislation did not call it a national park. It called Yellowstone the "nation's park." At the time, public sentiment favored giving away or privatizing the wilderness, not setting it aside, and somehow the term nation's park was a more politically palatable term than national park.

5. Yosemite National Park was established in 1890, but the National Park Service did not come into being until 1916. Woodrow Wilson signed a bill to approve construction of the O'Shaughnessy Dam in 1913, and the dam was completed ten years later.

6. This list of intangible human benefits comes from a longer list in a National Park Service training manual for interpreters. David L. Larsen, *Meaningful*

Interpretation: How to Connect Hearts and Minds to Places, Objects, and Other Resources (Washington, PA: Eastern National, 2003).

7. Ralph Waldo Emerson, *Nature* (Boston: James Munroe and Company, 1849).

8. Aldo Leopold, *A Sand County Almanac: With Essays on Conservation from Round River* (New York: Sierra Club/Ballantine, 1966), 138.

9. Although the US Forest Service no longer kills top predators to increase the size of its deer herd, it remains, like most natural resource management agencies, a conservation-oriented organization. The National Forest Management Act legislates that the Forest Service focus on timber, grazing, water, recreation, and wildlife. The one agency with a preservationist mission is the National Park Service. It has only two mandates, preservation and recreation, and when preservation and recreation conflict, preservation takes precedence. The Park Service operates for the protection of nature, but also for those human values we have a hard time getting a handle on—solitude, challenge, self-confidence, peace, freedom, nostalgia, spiritual growth, and the feeling of being a part of a place.

10. This viewpoint is described in William R. Jordan III, *The Sunflower Forest: Ecological Restoration and the New Communion with Nature* (Berkeley: University of California Press, 2003), 30–32.

11. In the United States, approximately 4 percent of the population hunts. In Wisconsin, the percentage is about 8 percent. Even with these relatively small numbers, hunting remains part of the state's culture.

12. Although the students came up with this insight on their own, it also comes straight out of *A Sand County Almanac*. Leopold wrote, "A peculiar virtue in wildlife ethics is that the hunter ordinarily has no gallery to applaud or disapprove of his conduct." Aldo Leopold, *A Sand County Almanac and Sketches Here and There* (London: Oxford University Press, 1949), 178.

13. I found out later that some hunters do eat sandhill cranes, but I didn't know it at the time. Wisconsin has added a mourning dove hunting season, but sandhill cranes remain a protected species. Almost every legislative session, a pro-hunting legislator reintroduces a bill to mandate sandhill crane hunting, but so far all efforts to this end have failed.

Chapter 18

1. Climber Stewart Green said, "Climbing may be hard, but it's easier than growing up." Stewart Green, "Climbing Quotes," Goodreads, https://www.good reads.com/quotes/tag/climbing?page=2.

2. There a several books by Csikszentmihalyi about flow. Some are too technical for my tastes. I like best the one that is just titled *Flow*. Mihaly Csikszentmihalyi, *Flow: The Psychology of Optimal Experience* (New York: Harper and Row, 1990).

Chapter 19

1. Emerson expressed this idea most explicitly in the essay "The Over-Soul," where he wrote, "We see the world piece by piece, as the sun, the moon, the animal, the tree; but the whole, of which these are the shining parts, is the soul." Ralph Waldo Emerson, *Essays* (New York: John B. Alden, 1885), 239.

2. Joseph Cornell, *Sharing Nature with Children* (Nevada City, CA: Dawn Publications, 1979).

3. Wes Jackson, *Becoming Native to This Place: The Blazer Lectures for 1991* (Lexington: University of Kentucky Press, 1994), 97.

4. Henry D. Thoreau, *The Illustrated Walden* (Princeton: Princeton University Press, 1973), 3.

5. Annie Dillard, *Pilgrim at Tinker Creek* (Toronto: Bantam Books, 1974), 12.

6. This Muir quote shows up on posters and the covers of blank journals, but its source is unclear. It does appear in the Muir biography *Son of the Wilderness*. Linnie Marsh Wolfe, *Son of the Wilderness: The Life of John Muir* (New York: A. A. Knopf, 1945).

7. Tim Patterson, "What Henry David Thoreau Taught Me about Travel," *Matador Network*, December 14, 2007, https://matadornetwork.com/bnt/what -henry-david-thoreau-taught-me-about-travel/.

8. For me, this statement is a paraphrase of the famous Muir quote, "I only went out for a walk and finally concluded to stay out till sundown, for going out, I found, was really going in." John Muir, *The Wilderness World of John Muir*, ed. Edwin Way Teale (Boston: Houghton Mifflin, 1954), 311.

9. As a kid, a crowded state park campground did not bother me. I was in nature. Now I'd rather stay at home than camp in a noisy campground. I'd like to believe the difference is a change of behavior in the modern-day camper, but I know the problem is with me.

10. When I tried to recall exceptional moments at Weborg Point, it was as if I'd opened a mental floodgate. In a few minutes I had a list of nearly two dozen memorable events (e.g., a porcupine in the same tree three years running, a tornado passing directly overhead, finding a four-leaf clover in the lawn outside the restrooms). I suspect most adults who had a special wild place as a kid can do the same.

Chapter 20

1. I was in attendance at this conference presentation, but do not remember the exact time or place. I was in graduate school, so it had to be the early 1980s. Ecofeminism was a fairly new concept at the time, and with her book *Green Paradise Lost*, Dodson Gray was considered one of the founders of the movement/philosophy.

2. Frederic Golden, "Albert Einstein," *Time*, December 31, 1999, http://content .time.com/time/magazine/article/0,9171,993017,00.html.

3. The integration of science and the humanities is not a new concept. The quote "You who honor both art and science" comes from Canto IV of Dante's *Inferno* (i.e., the fourteenth century). At this point in *Inferno*, Dante is in Limbo, encountering some of the greatest thinkers of all time (e.g., Homer, Ovid, Virgil). Dante is conflicted as to why these exceptional people who were brilliant in both the humanities and the sciences cannot get into Paradise just because they were pre-Christian. It was someone from the earliest years of the Renaissance wondering why scholars from the previous golden age were not venerated during the Middle Ages.

4. Thomas Berry, *The Dream of the Earth* (San Francisco: Sierra Club Books, 1988).

5. David Orr, *Earth in Mind: On Education, Environment, and the Human Prospect* (Washington, DC: Island Press, 1994), 44.

6. A prime example is recent scientific research confirming the benefits of time

in nature. Articles on this subject are many, one being Mathew P. White et al., "Spending at Least 120 Minutes a Week in Nature is Associated with Good Health and Wellbeing," *Scientific Reports* 9, no. 7730 (2019), https://doi.org/10.1038/s41598-019-44097-3.

7. Sara Moore, *Living Deliberately: Thoreau and Leisure* (La Crosse: University of Wisconsin–La Crosse Publications, 2014). As an aside, the philosophy professor in the anecdote was the same guy as the one who wandered the Italian countryside as a kid (see chapter 16) and taught ecological restoration (see chapter 21).

8. Alan Watts, in collaboration with Al Chung-liang Huang, *Tao: The Watercourse Way* (New York: Pantheon, 1975), 32.

9. Chung-ying Cheng, "On the Environmental Ethics of the Tao and the Ch'i," *Environmental Ethics* 8, no. 4 (Winter 1986): 351–70, https://doi.org/10.5840/enviroethics19868436.

10. Euglenas were also a problem because they seemed to be animals with chlorophyll. Since my childhood, other mobile creatures with chlorophyll have also been discovered.

11. There are several similar models to show the new thinking, but a good one can be found in Laura A. Hug et al., "A New View of the Tree of Life," *Natural Microbiology* 1 (2016), https://doi.org/10.1038/nmicrobiol.2016.48.

12. Mary Evelyn Tucker and Brian Thomas Swimme, "The Next Transition: The Evolution of Humanity's Role in the Universe," in *Spiritual Ecology: The Cry of the Earth*, ed. Llewelyn Vaughan-Lee (Point Reyes, CA: Golden Sufi Center, 2013), 55–66.

13. William R. Jordan III, *The Sunflower Forest: Ecological Restoration and the New Communion with Nature* (Berkeley: University of California Press, 2003), 14.

Chapter 21

1. I would argue that lots of trail construction, when done well, is ecological restoration. For example, my daughter, Clare, spent one summer working for the Wisconsin Conservation Corps. One of her crew's projects was on Lake Superior's Madeline Island. It was to build a boardwalk from the big lake to a much smaller lake a hundred yards inland. Sea kayakers had been landing

their boats on a long stretch of beach and, from wherever they came ashore, dragging their boats through an ecologically sensitive bog to get to the second body of water. The boardwalk preserved the bog by channeling these recreational boaters through a single designated access point. In my mind, the boardwalk was a form of ecological restoration.

2. The Wisconsin Conservation Corps, or WisCorps, is a nonprofit organizations that puts teenagers and young adults on various conservation projects around the state. It is modeled after the Civilian Conservation Corps of the 1930s and early 1940s, but unlike the old CCC, which used worthwhile conservation projects to give people jobs after the Great Depression, WisCorps uses similar conservation projects to offer youth an opportunity for public service. WisCorps's mission statement says nothing about restoring nature; it is entirely about developing youth. The exact wording of WisCorps's mission is "to develop leadership, self-confidence, and a strong work ethic in youth and young adults through the active stewardship of Wisconsin's communities and natural resources" (retrieved February 6, 2021, from www.wiscorps .org/about).

3. Goat prairies are small ecosystems unique to the Upper Mississippi River Valley. The south-facing sides of some of the bluffs are too steep, too dry, and too devoid of soil to support trees, so small shortgrass prairies form. Hixon Forest has a few healthy goat prairies.

4. One environmental issue in Hixon Forest is cowbird parasitism. Cowbirds lay eggs in the nests of other forest birds, often at the expense of the other young in the nest. Cowbirds, however, only invade nests on the edge of the forest or near a clearing. If an undisturbed forest is large enough, birds with nests deep in the forest do not suffer this kind of attack. Scott K. Robinson, et. al., "Management Implications of Cowbird Parasitism on Neotropical Migrant Songbirds," in *Status and Management of Neotropical Migratory Birds*, General Technical Report RM-229, ed. D. M. Finch and P. W. Stangel (Fort Collins, CO: US Department of Agriculture, Forest Service, Rocky Mountain Forest and Range Experiment Station, 1993), 93–102.

5. John Dewey, "The Duties and Responsibilities of the Teaching Profession,"

John Dewey: The Later Works, 1925-1953; Volume 5: 1929-1939, ed. Jo An Boyd-ston (Carbondale: Southern Illinois University Press, 1984), 326–30.

6. Sam drew many of his questions from philosophical writings, most notably William R. Jordan III, *The Sunflower Forest: Ecological Restoration and the New Communion with Nature* (Berkeley: University of California Press, 2003).

7. Demonstration plots are small areas meant to replicate natural ecosystems that might no longer exist in the immediate area. Arboretums, artificial ponds, and small prairies might all be demonstration plots.

8. Thomas Berry, *The Great Work: Our Way into the Future* (New York: Bell Tower, 1999), 3.

Epilogue

1. Tim Adams, "Zen and the Art of Following in Your Father's Footsteps," *Observer* (London), April 4, 2018, https://www.theguardian.com/books /2018/apr/04/zen-following-fathers-footsteps-peter-matthiessen-snow -leopard-40-years.

2. This is the final sentence of the Sierra Club/Ballantine version, but not the original Oxford University Press version. The final words of the Oxford University Press version are "We shall hardly relinquish the shovel, which after all has many good points, but we are in need of gentler and more objec-tive criteria for its successful use." To some extent, both closing sentences are saying the same thing. Aldo Leopold, *A Sand County Almanac: And Sketches Here and There* (London: Oxford University Press, 1949), 226, and Aldo Leo-pold, *A Sand County Almanac: With Essays on Conservation from Round River* (New York: Sierra Club/Ballantine, 1966), 295.

3. Clare graduated from Grinnell College a month after I wrote this epilogue. Two months after graduation she accepted an entry-level job at a green tech-nology firm. The company installs anaerobic digesters and devices that use natural gas more efficiently. Her work takes place in an office and not out-doors, but she probably will do more of Thomas Berry's Great Work than her dad ever did. Of course, I am very proud of her.

About the Author

STEVEN IS EMERITUS PROFESSOR OF RECREATION MANAGEMENT AT the University of Wisconsin–La Crosse. Over the years, he also has taught at National Taiwan University, Iowa State University, and the Graduate Institute of Environmental Education at National Taiwan Normal University. He lives in La Crosse, Wisconsin, with his wife, Manyu.